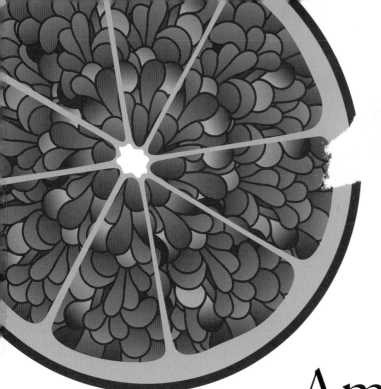

American English File

Student Book Starter

Clive Oxenden
Christina Latham-Koenig

OXFORD
UNIVERSITY PRESS

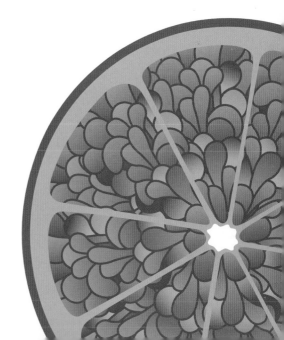

Paul Seligson and Clive Oxenden are the original co-authors of *English File 1* (pub. 1996) and *English File 2* (pub. 1997).

Contents

		Grammar	Vocabulary	Pronunciation

Look out for Study Link
This shows you where to find extra material for more practice and review.

G verb *be*: *I* and *you*
V numbers 0–10
P word stress; /h/, /oʊ/, and /ɑ/

Hi, I'm Henry. What's your name?

Hello!

1 LISTENING & SPEAKING

a **1.1** Listen and repeat.

Hi, I'm Molly.

Hi, I'm Henry.

Hello, I'm Linda Silva.

Hello, I'm Rob Jones.

b Now say who you are.

Hello, I'm _____.

c **1.2** Read and listen.

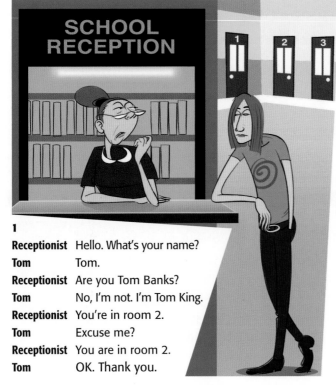

1

Receptionist	Hello. What's your name?
Tom	Tom.
Receptionist	Are you Tom Banks?
Tom	No, I'm not. I'm Tom King.
Receptionist	You're in room 2.
Tom	Excuse me?
Receptionist	You are in room 2.
Tom	OK. Thank you.

2

Tom	Excuse me.
Teacher	Hello. Are you Tom?
Tom	Yes. Nice to meet you.
Teacher	Nice to meet you.
Tom	Am I late?
Teacher	Yes, you are.
Tom	Sorry!

d **1.3** Listen and repeat dialogue **1**. In pairs, practice the dialogue.

e **1.4** Listen and repeat dialogue **2**. In pairs, practice the dialogue.

2 GRAMMAR verb *be*: *I* and *you*

a Look at dialogue **1** in **1c** on page 4. Complete the chart.

> I'm = I am
> You're = You _____

b → **p.88 Grammar Bank 1A.** Read the rules and do the exercises.

3 VOCABULARY numbers 0–10

a **1.6** Listen. What are the numbers?

b → **p.102 Vocabulary Bank** *Numbers.* Do part **A.**

c Count around the class from 0 to 10 and then from 10 to 0.

d **1.8** Listen and say the next number.

"*one, two*"

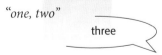
three

4 PRONUNCIATION word stress; /h/, /oʊ/, and /ɑ/

> **word stress: two-syllable words**
> LIsten   rePEAT

a **1.9** Match the words and photos. Listen and check.

☐ coffee ☐ photo ☐ e-mail ☐ hotel ☐ taxi

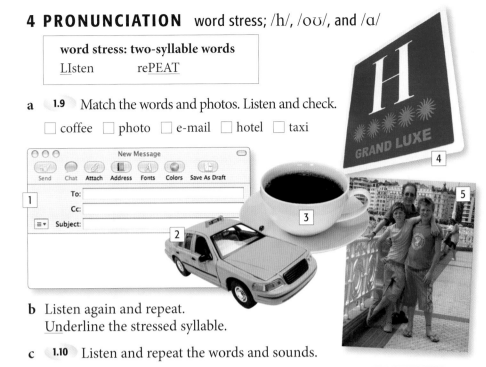
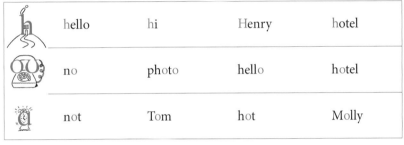

b Listen again and repeat. Underline the stressed syllable.

c **1.10** Listen and repeat the words and sounds.

	hello	hi	Henry	hotel
	no	photo	hello	hotel
	not	Tom	hot	Molly

d **1.11** Listen. Practice the sentences.

Hello. Henry's Hotel.
Oh, no! The phone!
Are you Molly? No. I'm not.

5 SPEAKING Practice with other students.

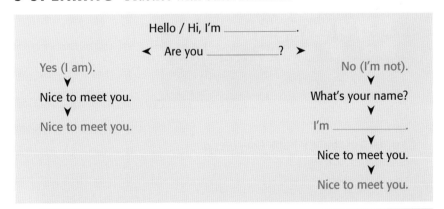

Hello / Hi, I'm _____.

◄ Are you _____? ►

Yes (I am).
▼
Nice to meet you.
▼
Nice to meet you.

No (I'm not).
▼
What's your name?
▼
I'm _____.
▼
Nice to meet you.
▼
Nice to meet you.

WORDS AND PHRASES TO LEARN		
He<u>llo</u>.	OK.	No.
Hi.	Thank you.	Nice to meet you.
What's your name?	<u>Ex</u>cuse me.	Am I late?
Ex<u>cuse</u> me?	Yes.	Sorry!

G verb *be*: *he, she, it*
V countries
P sentence stress; /ɪ/ and /aɪ/

> Where's he from?
> He's from Mexico.

Where are you from?

1 VOCABULARY countries

a Match the countries and photos.

Italy ☐   Japan ☐   Turkey ☐   Mexico ☐

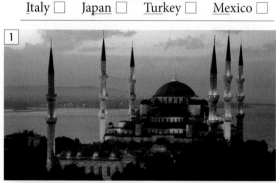

b **1.12** Listen and check.

c ➡ **p.103 Vocabulary Bank** *Countries and nationalities.* Do part **A**.

d **1.14** Listen and repeat the dialogue.

> **A** Where are you from?
> **B** I'm from Mexico.
> **A** Where in Mexico?
> **B** I'm from Mexico City.

e Practice the dialogue with your country and city.

2 GRAMMAR verb *be*: *he, she, it*

a **1.15** Listen and complete 1–3 with countries.

> **A** Where's he from?
> **B** He's from ¹ _____.
> **A** Is she from ² _____, too?
> **B** No, she isn't. She's from ³ _____.
> **A** Is it a good movie?
> **B** Yes, it is. It's great.

b **1.16** Listen and repeat.

c In pairs, practice the dialogue.

d Match the words and pictures.

| 1 | 2 | 3 |

she it he

_____   _____   _____

e ➡ **p.88 Grammar Bank 1B.** Read the rules and do the exercises.

3 PRONUNCIATION sentence stress; /ɪ/ and /aɪ/

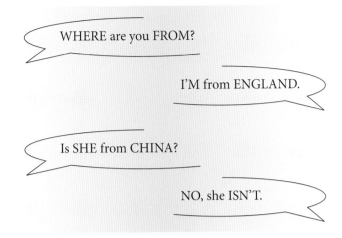

WHERE are you FROM?

I'M from ENGLAND.

Is SHE from CHINA?

NO, she ISN'T.

a Write sentences and questions.

1 / she / Brazil? No, / ___Is she from Brazil? No, she isn't.___

2 It / China. ___It's from China.___

3 She / Japan. _____

4 / he / Turkey? Yes, / _____

5 He / the United States. _____

6 / she / Mexico? No, / _____

7 She / England. _____

8 Where / he from? _____

  He / from Peru. _____

b **1.18** Listen and check.

c **1.19** Listen again and repeat. Copy the stress.

d **1.20** Listen and repeat the words and sounds.

🐟	it	Italy	six	Mexico	England
🚲	China	I	five	nine	hi	nice

e **1.21** Listen. Practice the sentences.

It's from Italy.
Liverpool is in England.
Hi. I'm from China. Nice to meet you.

4 LISTENING & SPEAKING

a **1.22** Listen. Can you hear the difference?

1	a Is he from Italy?	b Is she from Italy?
2	a She's from Russia.	b He's from Russia.
3	a Where's he from?	b Where's she from?
4	a It's from Korea.	b He's from Korea.
5	a She's late.	b He's late.
6	a Where is he?	b Where is she?

b **1.23** Listen and check (✔) the sentence you hear in **a**.

c Practice saying sentences a and b.

d Look at the photos. Guess the countries.
Ask your teacher.

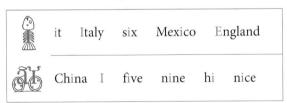

Is she from China?

**Famous actors in their countries –
but where are they from?**

e 🔵 **Communication** *Guess the countries A p.76 B p.78.*

WORDS AND PHRASES TO LEARN
Where are you from?
I'm from *Russia*.
Where in *Russia*?
I'm from *Moscow*.
Where is it?
Is it a good movie?
Yes, it's great.

1 C

G verb *be*: *we, you, they*; negatives (all persons)
V nationalities; numbers 11–20
P word stress; /ɛ/, /i/, and /ʃ/

> Are you Korean? Yes, we are.
> They aren't Spanish. They're Mexican.

We're from the US. We're American.

1 VOCABULARY nationalities

a Where are they from? Complete the sentences with a country.

1 I'm Japanese.

She's from _____ .

2 I'm American.

He's from _____ .

3 I'm Mexican.

She's from _____ .

4 I'm Turkish.

He's from _____ .

b 🔷 **p.103 Vocabulary Bank** *Countries and nationalities.* Do part **B**.

c **1.25** Listen. Say the nationality.

"I'm from Brazil."

She's Brazilian.

2 LISTENING & READING

a **1.26** Listen and number the pictures 1–3.

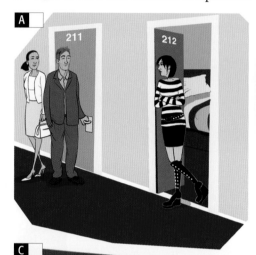

A

B

C

1

John	Hello. We're John and Sally Clarke.
Receptionist	Hello. You're in room 211, and they're in room 212.
Sally	Thank you.

2

| Sally | Hurry up. We're late. |
| Anna | We aren't late. Breakfast is from seven to ten. And Mike isn't ready. |

3

Liz	Hi. Are you American?
Mike	No, we aren't. We're English.
Liz	Are you on vacation?
Anna	Yes, we are.
Liz	We're on vacation, too. We're Liz and Travis, from Texas.
Travis	Bye. Have a nice day!
Anna	Good-bye.

b Listen again and read the dialogues. Then mark the sentences ✔ (right) or ✘ (wrong).

1 John and Sally are in room 212. ✘
2 Breakfast is from six to ten.
3 Mike and Anna aren't American.
4 Mike and Anna are English.
5 John and Sally are on vacation.
6 Liz and Travis aren't on vacation.

c Correct the wrong sentences.

John and Sally are in room 211.

d **1.27** Listen and repeat the dialogues.

3 GRAMMAR verb *be*: *we, you, they*; negatives (all persons)

a Read the dialogues in **2** on page 8 again. Complete the chart.

⊞	⊟
Singular	
I'm	*I'm not*
_____	You aren't
He's	_____
Plural	
We're	_____
_____	You aren't
_____	They aren't

b ⊙ **p.88 Grammar Bank 1C.** Read the rules and do the exercises.

c **1.29** Listen. Say the negative.

"*I'm Peruvian.*"

I'm not Peruvian.

4 PRONUNCIATION word stress; /ɛ/, /i/, and /ʃ/

a **1.30** The **same** stress or **different** stress? Listen and <u>underline</u> the stressed syllable. Write **S** or **D**.

1 Bra<u>zil</u>	Bra<u>zil</u>ian	*S*
2 <u>Chi</u>na	Chi<u>nese</u>	*D*
3 <u>Eng</u>land	<u>Eng</u>lish	___
4 <u>It</u>aly	I<u>tal</u>ian	___
5 <u>Rus</u>sia	<u>Rus</u>sian	___
6 <u>Mex</u>ico	<u>Mex</u>ican	___
7 Ja<u>pan</u>	Japa<u>nese</u>	___
8 <u>Tur</u>key	<u>Tur</u>kish	___

b Listen again and repeat.

c **1.31** Listen and repeat the words and sounds.

ɛ	Mexico	ten	seven	breakfast
i	we	he	she	meet	three
ʃ	she	Spanish	English	Russian	nationality

d **1.32** Listen. Practice the sentences.

Breakfast is from seven to ten.
He's Chinese.
She isn't Russian. She's Spanish.

5 SPEAKING

Are the nationalities right or wrong? Make ⊞ or ⊟ sentences. Correct the wrong nationalities.

Dim sum isn't Turkish. It's ...

dim sum / Turkish

Gisele Bündchen / Russian

The Rolling Stones / American

Andrea Bocelli / Brazilian

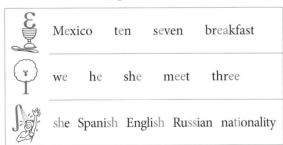
Corvettes / Italian

burritos / Spanish

Keira Knightley / British

Casio / Japanese

6 VOCABULARY numbers 11–20

a **1.33** Are they American or English? Listen and check. What are the numbers?

A

B

b ⊙ **p.102 Vocabulary Bank** *Numbers.* Do part **B**.

c Count in twos (*1, 3, 5…19* and *2, 4, 6…20*) around the class.

WORDS AND PHRASES TO LEARN
<u>Hurry</u> up.
<u>breakfast</u>
We're on va<u>ca</u>tion, too.
Good-<u>bye</u> / Bye.
Have a nice day!

The alphabet

How do you spell it? T-O-R-R-E-S.

1 LISTENING

a **1.35** Listen and order the sentences.

1

- ☐ This is the final call for passengers on Flight KLM 9246 to Miami. Please go to gate B14 immediately.
- ☐ Mr. Pablo Torres on Flight KLM 9246 to Miami, please go to gate B14 immediately.
- ☐ Passengers on Flight KLM 9246 to Miami, please go to gate B14.

2

- ☐ T-O-R-R-E-S.
- ☐ Hello. I'm Pablo Torres. I have a reservation.
- ☐ Excuse me?
- ☐ How do you spell your last name?
- ☐ Thank you.
- ☐ Good morning.
- ☐ T-O-R-R-E-S.

> first name = e.g., Brad, Keira
> last name = e.g., Pitt, Knightley

b **1.36** Listen and repeat dialogue **2**.

2 THE ALPHABET

a **1.37** Listen and repeat the words and sounds.

train	tree	egg	bike	phone	boot	car
A	B	F	I	O	Q	R
H	C	L	Y		U	
J	D	M			W	
K	E	N				
	G	S				
	P	X				
	T					
	V					
	Z					

b **1.38** Listen and repeat the letters.

c **1.39** Listen. Can you hear the difference?

| 1 M N | 3 G J | 5 Y I | 7 B V |
| 2 K Q | 4 E I | 6 U W | 8 E A |

d **1.40** Listen. Circle the letter you hear in **c**.

e **1.41** Listen and number the pictures 1–6.

f Listen again and write the letters. Practice saying them.

g **1.42** Listen and repeat the alphabet. Practice saying it.

A B C D E F G H I J K L M N O P Q R S T U V W X Y Z

h How do you spell the names?

| John | Sally | Liz | Anna | Mike | Travis |

3 PEOPLE ON THE STREET

> 1 What's your name?
> 2 How do you spell it?
> 3 Where are you from?

a **1.43** Listen to the man. What's his name?

b **1.44** Listen and write his name.

His name's _____.

c **1.45** Listen. Where's he from?

He's from Queens, _____.

d **1.46** Listen to six more people and complete the chart.

1 Her name's _____. She's from Los Angeles, _____.
2 Her name's _____. She's from Reading in _____.
3 His name's _____. He's from _____ in the US.
4 Her name's _____. She's from _____.
5 Her name's _____. She's from Bangalore, _____.
6 His name's _____. He's from Vancouver in _____.

e In pairs, ask and answer the questions in the box.

4 SPEAKING

Good morning	→ 12:00
Good afternoon	12:00 → 6:00 p.m.
Good evening	6:00 p.m. →

a In pairs, role-play dialogue **2** from exercise **1** on page 10.

A You're the receptionist. It's 4:00 p.m.
B Use your first and last name.

b Change roles.

B You're the receptionist. It's 7:00 p.m.
A Use your first and last name.

c ⬤ **Communication** *Game: Hit the ships A p.76 B p.79.*

5 VOCABULARY Classroom language

a ⬤ **p.104 Vocabulary Bank** *Things.* Do part **A**.

b Match the phrases and pictures.

☐ Close the door.
☐ Sit down, please.
☐ Look at the board, please.
☐ Go to page 14.
☐ Stand up.
☐ Open your books.

c **1.48** Listen and check. Listen again and repeat.

d **1.49** Listen and do the actions.

6 **1.50 SONG** ♫ *D-I-S-C-O*

WORDS AND PHRASES TO LEARN
Good <u>mor</u>ning / after<u>noon</u> / <u>eve</u>ning.
What's your last name?
How do you spell it?
Please.
I have a reser<u>va</u>tion.

GRAMMAR

Circle the correct answer.

Hello, ____ Alex.
a I   (b) I'm

1 ____ you from Brazil?
a Are   b Is

2 A Is Tom English?   B No, ____ American.
a she's   b he's

3 A ____ from?   B I'm from Korea.
a Where you are   b Where are you

4 A Are you in room 211?   B No, ____ in room 212.
a we're   b are

5 A Is Carmen Spanish?   B Yes, ____.
a she's   b she is

6 They ____ Chinese. They're Japanese.
a aren't   b are'nt

7 ____ Cancun in Mexico?
a Are   b Is

8 Lisa and Luke are from California. ____ American.
a You're   b They're

9 A Are you in class 2?   B No, ____.
a I not   b I'm not

10 She ____ from Chicago. She's from Los Angeles.
a aren't   b isn't

VOCABULARY

a Complete the chart.

Country	Nationality
Mexico	Mexican
China	1 _____
2 _____	Italian
England	3 _____
Brazil	4 _____
5 _____	American

b Write the next number.

one, two, *three*

1 six, seven, _____
2 two, one, _____
3 ten, eleven, _____
4 fifteen, fourteen, _____
5 eighteen, nineteen, _____

c Complete the phrases.

Where are you *from*?
A Excuse ¹ _____, are you Henry?
B Yes, I am.
A I'm Jim Brown. Nice to ² _____ you.

A ³ _____ afternoon. I'm Ann Carter.
I ⁴ _____ a reservation.
B Excuse me, how do you ⁵ _____ your last name?
A C-A-R-T-E-R.

d Write the things in the classroom.

1 _____

2 _____

3 _____

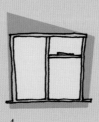

4 _____   5 _____

PRONUNCIATION

a Can you remember these words and sounds?

vowels   consonants

b ⏵ **p.117 / 119 Sound Bank.** Check the words and sounds, and practice saying the example words.

c Underline the stressed syllable.
Italian

Japan   Japanese   hotel   sorry   American

What can you do?

1 CAN YOU UNDERSTAND THIS TEXT?

Read and complete the chart for Marta, Jian-hao, and Kelly.

I'm Marta Ramírez.
I'm from Monterrey in Mexico.

I'm Jian-hao Li.
I'm from Shanghai in China.

I'm Kelly Doyle.
I'm from Kansas in the United States.

	First name	Last name	Nationality
	Marta		
	Jian-hao		
	Kelly		
You			

2 CAN YOU WRITE THIS IN ENGLISH?

a Complete the chart for you.

b Write two sentences about you.

3 CAN YOU UNDERSTAND THESE PEOPLE?

1.51 Listen and choose the right answer.

1 a Danny's American.   b Danny's English.
2 a Bella's in room 9.   b Bella's in room 19.
3 a She's Kathy.   b She's Cathy.
4 a The bus is number 13.   b The bus is number 14.
5 a Li-ming is from China.   b Li-ming is from Korea.
6 a The flight is UA472.   b The flight is UA462.
7 a He's John Read.   b He's John Reid.
8 a Chris is a woman.   b Chris is a man.
9 a The exercise is on page 11. b The exercise is on page 12.
10 a It's 8:00 a.m.   b It's 8:00 p.m.

4 CAN YOU SAY THIS IN ENGLISH?

Check (✔) the boxes.
Can you…?

say your name and where you are from	☐ Yes, I can.
ask where other people are from	☐ Yes, I can.
spell your name	☐ Yes, I can.
count from 0 to 20	☐ Yes, I can.
check in at a hotel	☐ Yes, I can.

2 A

G singular and plural nouns; *a / an, the*
V small things
P /z/ and /s/, plural endings

> What are they? They're keys.

What's in your bag?

1 VOCABULARY small things

a Can you remember five things in the classroom? Write the words.

1 the **b**_____ 2 the **d**_____ 3 a **c**_____ 4 a **l**_____ 5 a **w**_____

b ➲ **p.104 Vocabulary Bank** *Things.* Do part **B**.

2 GRAMMAR singular and plural nouns; *a / an, the*

a Read and order the things (bags, coats, etc.) 1–5.

Where is it? Oh, no! It's on the train!

The **top five** things people leave on British trains are (not in order):

- ☐ bags
- ☐ coats
- ☐ glasses
- ☐ cell phones
- ☐ umbrellas

b [2.2] Listen and check.

c Write the plurals.

1 bag _____*bags*_____
2 chair _____
3 book _____
4 laptop _____

d ➲ **p.90 Grammar Bank 2A.** Read the rules and do the exercises.

e ➲ **Communication** *Memory game p.81.*

3 PRONUNCIATION /z/ and /s/, plural endings

a [2.4] Listen and repeat the words and sounds.

Brazil	zero	is	he's
six	seven	Spain	house

b [2.5] Listen and repeat the plurals.

chairs	photos	keys	bags
books	coats	laptops	clocks
/ɪz/ watches	buses	pieces	classes

c [2.6] Listen. Say the plurals.

"It's a photo."

> They're photos.

4 SPEAKING & WRITING

a Ask and answer with a partner.

> What is it?

> It's a / an…

> What are they?

> They're…

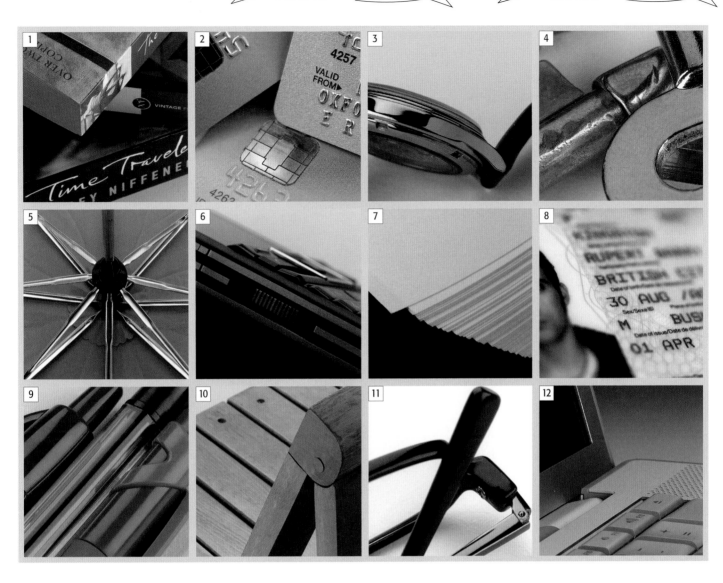

b What's in your bag / pocket? Check (✔) the things.

a cell phone ☐
a book ☐
a key ☐
an ID card ☐
a photo ☐
an umbrella ☐
glasses ☐
a credit card ☐
a pen ☐

c Write what you have in your bag / pocket, e.g., a book, keys.

d Now tell a partner.

> In my bag, I have a book, keys, a pen, …

5 LISTENING

2.7 Listen to five conversations. Write the thing or things that they say.

1 Is this your _____?
2 Here are your _____.
3 Sorry, it's my _____.
4 Look in the _____.
5 Is a _____ _____ OK?

WORDS AND PHRASES TO LEARN
What is it?
What are they?
What's in your bag?
I have *two credit cards*.

G possessive adjectives; possessive *s*
V people and family
P /ð/, /ʌ/, and /ə/

Family and friends

> Who's Maria?
> She's my brother's wife.

1 GRAMMAR possessive adjectives

a **2.8** Listen. Number the pictures 1–3.

DETROIT flight AA4874

1
A Hey! That's my bag.
B No, it isn't. It's my bag. Your bag's there.

2
A And here are our children.
B What are their names?
A Her name's Lucy, and his name's Eric.
B Hello. And who's this?
C It's my parrot.
B What's its name?
C Polly.
B Hello, Polly.

3
A Where are our coats?
B Excuse me?
A Where are our coats?
B Your coats – they're over there on the chair.
A Thank you. Good night.
B Bye.

b Listen again and read the dialogues. Then complete the chart with a highlighted word.

I	*my* (bag)	we	_____
you	_____	you	_____
he	_____	they	_____
she	_____		
it	_____		

c ➡ **p.90 Grammar Bank 2B.** Read the rules for possessive adjectives. Do exercise **a**.

d Talk to a partner. Point to people in the classroom. Can you remember their names?

> What's her name?

> I can't remember. What are their names?

2 VOCABULARY people and family

a Look at pictures A–C. Where can you see…?
a man, a woman, and two children ☐
men and women ☐
two boys ☐

b ➡ **p.105 Vocabulary Bank** *People and family*.

3 PRONUNCIATION /ð/, /ʌ/, and /ə/

a **2.13** Listen and repeat the words and sounds.

	father	they	their	the
	brother	husband	son	mother
	pocket	seven	woman	children

b **2.14** Listen. Practice the sentences.

The woman over there is my mother.
I have one brother and three sons.
My husband and I have seven children.

4 GRAMMAR possessive *s*

a Match the pairs from five famous movies.

A Miranda

B Captain Teague

C Leia

D Pam

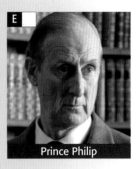
E Prince Philip

1 Bridget

2 the Queen

3 Carrie

4 Jack Sparrow

5 Luke

b Complete the sentences with a name.

1 _____ is Carrie's friend.

2 _____ is Bridget's mother.

3 _____ is Jack Sparrow's father.

4 _____ is Luke's sister.

5 _____ is the Queen's husband.

c **2.15** Listen and check.

d ◯ **p.90 Grammar Bank 2B.** Read the rules for possessive *s*. Do exercise **b**.

e Cover **b** and practice with photos A–E. Ask and answer.

Who's Miranda? She's …

f Work with a partner:

A and B write the names of six people (your family or friends) on a piece of paper.

A give your piece of paper to **B**. **B** give your piece of paper to **A**.

A ask **B** about his / her people. **B** ask **A** about his / her people.

Who's Silvia? She's my sister.

5 WRITING & SPEAKING

a Read the text and write the names on the photo.

Kate

My name is Kate. I'm from Ohio in the United States. My father's name is Marty, and my mother's name is Amy. I have a brother and a sister. Their names are Brett and Karen. We have a dog. Its name is Brandy.

b Now write about your family.

c Tell your partner about your family.

WORDS AND PHRASES TO LEARN	
That's *my bag.*	Who's this?
here	I can't re<u>me</u>mber.
there	Thanks.
<u>o</u>ver there	

2C

G adjectives
V colors and common adjectives
P /æ/, /eɪ/, /ɔ/, /ɑr/, and /ɔr/

A man's car or a woman's car?

> It's a fast car.

1 VOCABULARY & SPEAKING colors and common adjectives

a **2.17** Match the cars and nationalities. Listen and check.

American ☐
British ☐
French ☐
German ☐
Italian ☐
Japanese ☐

b **2.18** Listen and read the dialogue. What are the two cars?

Tim Wow! Look at that car. It's great!
Sue It's a man's car.
Tim A man's car?
Sue Yes. It's fast and red. And it's very expensive. Wow! Look at that yellow car. It's great!
Tim It's a woman's car.

c Look at the highlighted words. Guess their meaning.

d **2.19** Listen again and repeat the dialogue. Then practice it with a partner.

e ⊙ **p.106 Vocabulary Bank** *Adjectives*.

f Look at the photos of the cars 1–6. Practice with a partner.
1 Ask and answer.

> What color is it?
> It's ...

2 Describe the cars. Use two adjectives. *Car 2 is small and cheap.*
3 **A** think of a car. **B** ask questions. Guess the car.

> **B**
> Is it French?
> **A**
> No, it isn't.

2 GRAMMAR adjectives

a Circle the right sentence.
1 a The VW is a small car.
  b The VW is a car small.
2 a Ferraris and Mustangs are fasts cars.
  b Ferraris and Mustangs are fast cars.

b ⊙ **p.90 Grammar Bank 2C.** Read the rules and do the exercises.

c ⊙ **p.106 Vocabulary Bank** *Adjectives*. In pairs, look at the pictures and make ten sentences.

> It's a big house.
> They're blue keys.

3 READING

a With a partner, decide which questions you think are important for men and which are important for women. Write 1–7 in the article.

1 Is it a nice color?
2 Is it fast?
3 Is it big?
4 Is it cheap?
5 Is it easy to park?
6 Is it luxurious?
7 Is it safe?

b Read the article and check.

What car? Men and women are different.

Important questions for men:

_____? _____? _____?

Important questions for women:

___1___? _____? _____? _____?

Mercedes, BMW, and Audi are very popular with men. 90% of drivers of the luxurious Mercedes S65 AMG (top speed 155 mph) are men. Big SUVs are also very popular with men.

Honda, Hyundai, and Volkswagen are popular with women. 65% of drivers of VW Beetle convertibles are women. Three of the top five women's cars are sports cars (but not very expensive sports cars). Women prefer cars that are small (easy to park) and safe. Color is also very important.

4 PRONUNCIATION /æ/, /eɪ/, /ɔ/, /ɑr/, and /ɔr/

a **2.24** Listen and repeat the words and sounds.

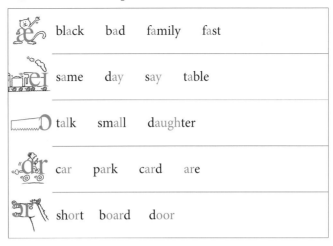

æ	black	bad	family	fast
eɪ	same	day	say	table
ɔ	talk	small	daughter	
ɑr	car	park	card	are
ɔr	short	board	door	

b **2.25** Listen. Practice the phrases.

a black cat
the same day
a small ball
park the car
a short door

5 SPEAKING & WRITING

a Talk in small groups about your car or your family's car.

> My car is a Honda Civic. It's small, it's green, and it's new. It's a very good car.

b Write about your "dream" car.

My dream car is a _____. (model) It's a / an _____ car. (nationality)
It's _____. (color) It's _____ and _____. (adjectives)

c Now tell a partner.

6 **2.26** SONG ♫ *You're beautiful*

WORDS AND PHRASES TO LEARN	
German (country = Germany)	Wow!
French (country = France)	also
Look at *that car*!	important
easy (opposite = difficult)	popular
safe (opposite = dangerous)	with
What's your favorite *car*?	

2

PRACTICAL
ENGLISH

Introducing people
Phone numbers

Numbers 21–100
Personal information: age, address, etc.

How old is he? He's 26.

Personal information

1 INTRODUCING PEOPLE

a **2.27** Listen to two dialogues. Mark the sentences T (true) or F (false).

Dialogue 1 Helen is Mike's sister. ☐
Dialogue 2 The girl's brother is 25. ☐

1
A Hello, Mike.
B _____, Sam. How are you?
A Fine, thanks. And _____?
B I'm OK, thanks. This is Helen. She's a _____ from work.
A _____ to meet you.
C Hi.
B _____, we're in a hurry. See you soon. Bye.
A _____.

2
A Look. This is my _____.
B Wow! He's _____ good-looking. What's his _____?
A Adam.
B _____ he married?
A No, he isn't.
B How old is he?
A _____ twenty-six.
B What's his _____ number?

b Listen again and read. Complete the dialogues.

c **2.28** Listen and repeat the dialogues.

d Practice them with a partner.

2 VOCABULARY
phone numbers, 21–100

> **Phone numbers**
> 0 = oh (or zero)

a **2.29** Listen to the dialogue and write the phone number.

A What's your phone number?
B __ __ __   __ __ __ - __ __ __ __
A Excuse me?

b **2.30** Practice saying these phone numbers. Listen and check.
1 **688-5713**
2 **844-7902**
3 **231 555-0261**

c In pairs, practice the dialogue in **a**. Use your phone number (or an invented number).

d ⊙ **p.102 Vocabulary Bank** *Numbers*. Do part **C**.

e **2.32** Listen. Can you hear the difference?
	a		b	
1	a	13	b	30
2	a	14	b	40
3	a	15	b	50
4	a	16	b	60
5	a	17	b	70
6	a	18	b	80
7	a	19	b	90

f **2.33** Listen and circle a or b. Then practice saying all the numbers.

g How old are the people in your family?

> My mother's 54.

> **Ages**
> He's 20 OR He's 20 years old.
> NOT ~~He's 20 years~~, ~~He has 20 years~~

3 PEOPLE ON THE STREET 🖥

Matthew

> 1 Do you have brothers and sisters?
> 2 How old are they? How old is he / she?

a 2.34 Listen to Matthew. Does he have brothers and sisters?

b 2.35 Listen. How old are they?

c 2.36 Listen to six more people. Answer the questions for each person.

	Elena	Hampton	Jared	Lauren	Sohail	Anna
Brothers and sisters?						
How old?						

d In pairs, ask and answer the questions in the box.

4 PERSONAL INFORMATION

a 2.37 Listen and repeat questions 1–9. Stress the underlined words.

1 What's your name? How do you spell it?
2 Where are you from?
3 What's your address?
4 What's your zip code?
5 How old are you?
6 Are you married?
7 What's your home phone number?
8 What's your cell phone number?
9 What's your e-mail address?

Immigration form

1 First name _____ Last name _____ *Title Mr. / Ms. / Mrs.
2 Nationality _____
3 Address _____
4 Zip code _____
5 Age _____
6 Married ☐ Single ☐
7 Phone number: home _____
8 cell _____
9 E-mail address _____

* Mr. = a man; Ms. = a woman; Mrs. = a married woman

b Cover the questions and look at the form. Remember the questions.

c Complete the form for you. Circle your title, too.

d ⊙ **Communication** *Personal information A p.77 B p.79.*

WORDS AND PHRASES TO LEARN

How are you?
  Fine, thanks. And you?
I'm OK, thanks.
This is *Helen.*
See you soon.
We're in a hurry.

What's your phone number?
What's your (e-mail) address?
How old are you?
  I'm *18.*
Are you *married*?

GRAMMAR

Circle the correct answer.

Hello, _____ Alex.
a I   (b) I'm

1 **A** What is it?
   B It's _____ e-mail from my friend.
   a an   b a

2 **A** Where's your ID card?
   B _____ in my bag.
   a Is   b It's

3 **A** What are they?
   B _____.
   a They're credit cards   b It's a credit card

4 I have two _____.
   a dictionarys   b dictionaries

5 She's American. _____ name is Julia.
   a Her   b His

6 We're Mr. and Mrs. Kemp. _____ daughter is in class 3.
   a Our   b Their

7 My _____ is Peter.
   a name's husband   b husband's name

8 These chairs are _____.
   a very expensive   b very expensives

9 A Ferrari is a _____.
   a car fast   b fast car

10 That's my sister and _____ boyfriend.
   a her   b their

VOCABULARY

a Write the things.

1 *a photo*   2 _____

3 _____   4 _____

5 _____   6 _____

b Complete the chart.

👤	👩
man	*woman*
father	1 _____
2 _____	wife
son	3 _____
4 _____	sister
boyfriend	5 _____

c Write the irregular plural.

man	*men*
1 woman	_____
2 child	_____
3 person	_____

d Write the opposite adjective.

fast	*slow*
1 expensive	_____
2 big	_____
3 good	_____
4 long	_____
5 tall	_____

e Write the number.

thirty-one   *31*   3 ninety-nine _____
1 forty   ___   4 fifty-six ___
2 sixty-seven ___   5 eighty-two ___

f Complete the phrases.

Where are you *from*?

1 **A** _____ is my sister Anne.   **B** Nice to meet you.
2 **A** How _____ is Rita?   **B** I think she's 22.
3 **A** How are you?   **B** _____, thanks. And you?
4 **A** Where's my book?   **B** It's _____ there on the table.
5 **A** What's your _____?   **B** 25 King Street.

PRONUNCIATION

a Can you remember these words and sounds?

vowels

consonants

b ➲ **p.117 / 119 Sound Bank.** Check the words and sounds, and practice saying the example words.

c Underline the stressed syllable.

Italian

| expensive | daughter | family | glasses | umbrella |

1 CAN YOU UNDERSTAND THIS TEXT?

My name's Elena Flores, and I'm from Mendoza in Argentina. I'm married, and I have two children, a son and a daughter. My son's name is Victor. He's 15. He's tall with dark hair, and he's good-looking. My daughter's name is Carla. She's 21. Is she beautiful? I think she is very beautiful – I'm her mother!

My name's Greg, and I'm from Florida in the US. I'm 20. I have two sisters. Their names are Diane and Liz. Diane is 26. She's tall, with long blond hair. She's married. Her husband's name is Kyle. Liz is 19 and very different from Diane. She isn't tall and blond. She's short with dark hair. She isn't married, but she has a boyfriend!

a Read the two texts. Answer the questions with a sentence.

1 What's Elena's last name?   *Her last name is Flores.*
2 Where is Elena from? _____
3 How old is Victor? _____
4 What's her daughter's name? _____
5 What nationality is Greg? _____
6 Who is Diane? _____
7 Is she married or single? _____
8 How old is Liz? _____

b Look at the highlighted words. Use the photos to guess their meaning.

2 CAN YOU WRITE THIS IN ENGLISH?

Write about you and your family. Use *and* and *but* where necessary.

> **and / but**
> He's tall. He's good-looking. ➤ He's tall **and** good-looking.
> He's tall. He isn't good-looking. ➤ He's tall, **but** he isn't good-looking.

3 CAN YOU UNDERSTAND THESE PEOPLE?

2.38 Listen and choose the right answer.

1 a His name's Alex.
   b Her name's Alex.
2 a His glasses are blue.
   b His glasses are red.
3 a Her address is 19 Park Street.
   b Her address is 90 Park Street.
4 a The hotel's nice.
   b The hotel's very small.
5 a Her father is 67.
   b Her father is 76.
6 a His phone number is 771 555-7064.
   b His phone number is 771 555-7065.
7 a His sister is tall.
   b His sister is short.
8 a It's a CD.
   b It's a DVD.
9 a Her e-mail address is susie@gomail.com.
   b Her e-mail address is suzy@gomail.com.
10 a His car is white.
   b His car is black.

4 CAN YOU SAY THIS IN ENGLISH?

Check (✔) the boxes.
Can you…?

say what's in your bag	☐ Yes, I can.
say who is in your family	☐ Yes, I can.
describe your car	☐ Yes, I can.
count from 21 to 100	☐ Yes, I can.
introduce somebody	☐ Yes, I can.
ask how somebody is	☐ Yes, I can.
say your phone number	☐ Yes, I can.
ask for and give personal information, e.g., name, address, age, etc.	☐ Yes, I can.

3 A

G simple present: *I* and *you*
V common verbs 1
P /u/, /w/, and /v/; linking

> Do you live near here? No, I don't.

A bad hair day

1 LISTENING & READING

a **3.1** Listen to the dialogue. Number the pictures 1–5.

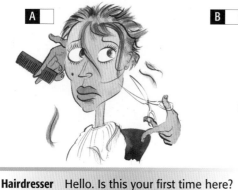

A ☐ **B** ☐ **C** ☐ **D** ☐ **E** ☐

Hairdresser	Hello. Is this your first time here?
Customer	Yes, it is.
Hairdresser	Do you live ¹ *near here*?
Customer	No, I don't. I live ² _____.
Hairdresser	Oh, nice. How do you want your hair?
Customer	I don't know. Something different.
Hairdresser	Do you want a ³ _____?
Customer	No, thanks. I don't drink ⁴ _____.
Hairdresser	Do you want a ⁵ _____?
Customer	Yes, please. Oh, look. Demi Moore's children.
Hairdresser	Do you have ⁶ _____?
Customer	Yes, I do. I have two ⁷ _____.
Hairdresser	How old are they?
Customer	Eight and ten.
Customer	It's very short.
Hairdresser	Don't worry. Wait.
Hairdresser	OK. Do you like it?

b Read the dialogue and complete 2–7 with a word(s) from the list.

boys   children   coffee (x2)   downtown   magazine   ~~near here~~

c Listen and check.

d ○ **Communication** *A new haircut p.81* Do you like her haircut?

e **3.2** Listen and complete the last line of the dialogue.

Hairdresser	OK. Do you like it?
Customer	_____

f Practice the dialogue with a partner.

2 GRAMMAR   simple present: *I* and *you*

a Read the dialogue again. Complete the chart with *do* or *don't*.

> **Simple present**
> ⊞ I live near here. ⊟ I _____ live near here.
> ? _____ you live near here?
> ✔ Yes, I _____. ✗ No, I _____.

b ○ **p.92 Grammar Bank 3A.** Read the rules and do the exercises.

3 VOCABULARY   common verbs 1

a Match the phrases.

1 I have *b*   a downtown.
2 I drink ☐   b two children.
3 I live ☐   c coffee.
4 I want ☐   d my new haircut.
5 I like ☐   e a magazine.

b ○ **p.107 Vocabulary Bank** *Common verbs 1.*

4 LISTENING

a **3.6** Listen to the dialogue. Is the woman happy ☺ or sad ☹ at the end of the dialogue?

b Listen again. What do the woman and taxi driver say? Circle a or b.

1 a Geary Street, please.
  b Kearny Street, please.

2 a The traffic is bad.
  b The traffic is good.

3 a Do you live in San Francisco?
  b Do you like San Francisco?

4 a What's the problem?
  b No problem.

5 a I like my new haircut.
  b I don't like my new haircut.

6 a Why not? I like it.
  b Why not? It's fantastic.

7 a Where do you want to go?
  b Where do you want to stop?

8 a I want a new coat.
  b I want a new bag.

9 a That's 14.50.
  b That's 16.00.

10 a Have a good day.
   b Have a nice day.

5 PRONUNCIATION
/u/, /w/, and /v/; linking

a **3.7** Listen and repeat the words and sounds.

![u]	do	you	food	too	
![w]	watch	want	where	what	work
![v]	have	live	very	TV	

b **3.8** Listen and repeat. Link the words.

A Do you live in an apartment?
B No, I don't. I live in a house.
A Do you have children?
B Yes, I do. I have a boy and a girl.

6 SPEAKING

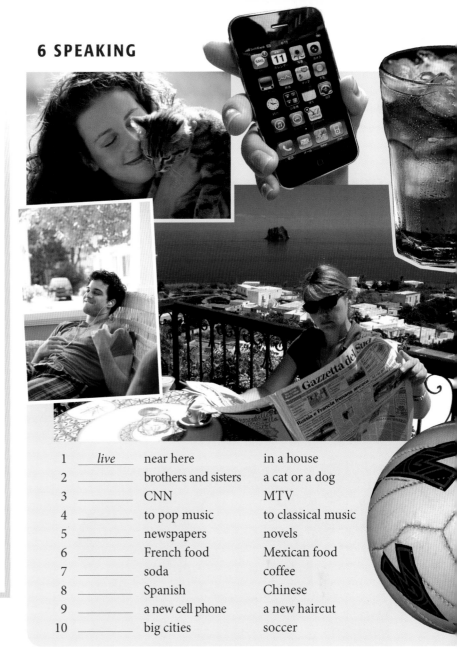

1	_live_	near here	in a house
2	_____	brothers and sisters	a cat or a dog
3	_____	CNN	MTV
4	_____	to pop music	to classical music
5	_____	newspapers	novels
6	_____	French food	Mexican food
7	_____	soda	coffee
8	_____	Spanish	Chinese
9	_____	a new cell phone	a new haircut
10	_____	big cities	soccer

a Complete 2–10 with a verb from the list.

drink eat have like listen ~~live~~ read speak want watch

b Work with a partner. Ask and answer with *Do you...?*

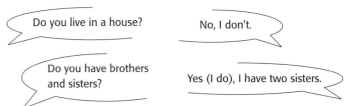

Do you live in a house?

No, I don't.

Do you have brothers and sisters?

Yes (I do), I have two sisters.

WORDS AND PHRASES TO LEARN

I don't know.	Wait.
Do you want *a coffee*?	Are you OK?
Yes, please.	What's the <u>problem</u>?
No, thanks.	<u>Really</u>?
Don't <u>worry</u>.	

G simple present: *we, you, they*
V food and drink
P word stress; /tʃ/, /dʒ/, and /g/

> Do you have coffee for breakfast?
> No, we don't. We have green tea.

What do you have for breakfast?

1 VOCABULARY food and drink

a Read the text and label the picture.

Anne from Paris in France

I don't have breakfast at home. I have it in a cafe. I have a croissant and hot chocolate. I think that's a very typical French breakfast. And it's very good!

b ⬦ **p.108 Vocabulary Bank** *Food and drink.*

2 READING

a Look at the photos. What food can you see?

Ken from Osaka in Japan

In my family, we have a traditional Japanese breakfast. It isn't very different from lunch and dinner. We have rice, fish, and miso soup, and we drink green tea. Today a lot of Japanese people have a Western breakfast. They have bread and croissants, and they drink coffee, not tea. But I prefer our breakfast. In my family, we don't talk at breakfast. We eat, drink, and watch TV!

Kendra from Chicago in the US

In the United States, we usually have a small breakfast during the week and a big breakfast on the weekend. In my family, we have eggs, potatoes, and sausage on Saturday. We also have bread—usually toast. We drink coffee and fruit juice. I like black coffee. It's very strong. My sister likes coffee with milk and sugar.

b Read the texts. Then read sentences 1–5 and mark the sentences T (true) or F (false).

1 In Japan, people eat very different things for breakfast, lunch, and dinner.
2 Ken's family likes croissants for breakfast.
3 In Japan, a lot of people don't have a traditional breakfast.
4 In the US, people eat a lot for breakfast during the week.
5 Kendra's family has a big breakfast on Saturday.

c Look at the highlighted words. Use the photos to guess their meaning.

d What do you have for breakfast?

3 GRAMMAR simple present: *we, you, they*

a Look at the sentences. Are the verbs the same or different for *I*, *we*, and *they*?

> **I have** a croissant for breakfast.
> **We have** a traditional Japanese breakfast.
> **They have** eggs and cheese for breakfast.

b ⊙ **p.92 Grammar Bank 3B.** Read the rules and do the exercises.

4 LISTENING

a **3.11** Listen to William on a British radio show called *You are what you eat*. What's his favorite meal?

b Listen again. Check (✔) the things he has:

Breakfast:
bread butter croissant cereal tea coffee

Breakfast on the weekend:
eggs potatoes vegetables sausage toast

Lunch:
a sandwich a pizza a hamburger water soda juice

Dinner:
meat rice pasta fish salad vegetables potatoes

c ⊙ **p.83.** Listen again with the script. Check your answers to **b**.

d What's your favorite meal of the day?

5 PRONUNCIATION
word stress; /tʃ/, /dʒ/, and /g/

a **3.12** Underline the stressed syllable. Listen and check.

vegetables	potatoes	butter	sugar
salad	cereal	chocolate	

b **3.13** Listen and repeat the words and sounds.

tʃ	cheese	lunch	chocolate	sandwich
dʒ	juice	Japan	orange	vegetables
g	sugar	eggs	go	bag

c **3.14** Listen. Practice the sentences.

I'm Charlie. I have a cheese sandwich for lunch.
I'm Jane. I drink orange juice for breakfast.
I'm Grace. I have eggs and tea with sugar.

6 SPEAKING & WRITING

a Read the questionnaire and think about your answers.

FOOD QUESTIONNAIRE

In your country…
What do people have for breakfast?
Do people prefer tea or coffee?
Do they have a big meal for lunch or for dinner?
Do they eat a lot of fruit and vegetables?
Do they eat a lot of fast food?

In your family…
What do you have for breakfast on the weekend?
What do you usually drink with lunch and dinner?
Do you eat a lot of rice?
Do you eat a lot of pasta?
Do you eat a lot of potatoes?
Do you eat a lot of meat?
Do you eat a lot of fish?
Do you have dinner together?
Do you watch TV or talk?

b Ask and answer the questions with a partner.

c Write about people from your country and your family.

> *Breakfast*
>
> *In my country*
> *In _____, people usually have _____ or _____ for breakfast. They don't have _____ or _____. They drink _____ or _____.*
>
> *In my family*
> *We usually have _____ for breakfast. On the weekend we have _____.*

WORDS AND PHRASES TO LEARN
I pre**fer** *our traditional breakfast.*
on the weekend
at home / at work
It de**pends**.
a lot of
For breakfast I have…
to**get**her

3C

G simple present: *he, she, it*
V jobs and places of work
P 3rd person *s*; word and sentence stress

What does she do? She's a doctor.
Where does she work? She works in a hospital.

He speaks English at work

1 GRAMMAR simple present: *he, she, it*

a **3.15** Listen to the dialogue. Circle a or b.

1 a Sofia and her husband live in the US.
  b Sofia and her husband live in Mexico.
2 a Sofia's husband is a teacher.
  b Sofia's husband is a tour guide.
3 a They like their jobs.
  b They don't like their jobs.

b Listen again and read the dialogue. Check your answers.

Emily Your English is fantastic. What do you do?
Sofia I'm a teacher. I teach English at a university here in Mexico City.
Emily Do you like your job?
Sofia Yes, I like it very much.
Emily What does your husband do?
Sofia He's a tour guide. He works at the National Museum of Art.
Emily Does he like his job?
Sofia Yes, very much. He likes art and history. And he doesn't work in the morning, only in the afternoon.
Emily Does he speak English, too?
Sofia Yes, he does. He speaks it very well. He meets a lot of American and British tourists.
Emily Do you speak English together?
Sofia Only when we don't want our children to understand!

c **3.16** Listen and repeat the highlighted phrases. How do the verbs change when they are about Sofia's husband? Complete the chart.

I / you	he / she
What **do you** do?	What _____ **your husband** do?
Do you like your job?	_____ **he** like his job?
Yes, **I like** it very much.	Yes, **he** _____ art and history.

d ➡ p.92 Grammar Bank 3C. Read the rules and do the exercises.

2 PRONUNCIATION 3rd person *s*

a **3.18** Listen and repeat the words and sounds.

	does	has	lives	listens	reads
	likes	speaks	works	eats	drinks
/ɪz/	finishes	watches	teaches		

b **3.19** Listen. Say the sentences in the 3rd person singular.

"I like art. He…"   He likes art.

3 VOCABULARY
jobs and places of work

a Can you remember? What does Sofia do? What does her husband do?

b ⊙ **p.109 Vocabulary Bank** *Jobs and places of work.*

c Ask five other students *What do you do?*

4 PRONUNCIATION
word and sentence stress

a Underline the stressed syllable(s).

1 a teacher
2 a doctor
3 a waiter
4 a factory worker
5 an assistant
6 a policeman
7 a salesperson
8 a lawyer

b **3.23** Listen and check. How is the final *-er* / *-or* pronounced?

c **3.24** Listen and repeat. Copy the rhythm.

She's a nurse. She works in a hospital.
Does he work in a store? Yes, he does.
Is he a salesperson? Yes, he is.

5 SPEAKING & WRITING

a Think of two people you know who have jobs. Ask and answer with a partner.

What / do?
 Where / work?
  / speak English at work?
  / like his/her job?

Person number one is my mother.

What does she do?

b Write about the two people.

My mother is a nurse. She works in the Hospital Santa Cruz in Curitiba. She doesn't speak English at work. She likes her job.

6 READING

a Is English important for these jobs in your town / city? Write 1–5 in the boxes (1 = English is not important, 5 = English is <u>very</u> important).

a waiter ☐ a doctor ☐ a taxi driver ☐ a policeman ☐ a teacher ☐ a lawyer ☐

b Read the text. Then answer the questions.

1 What do the banker, the waiter, and the factory worker have in common?
2 What does Jean-Paul do?
3 Where does he work?
4 What languages does he speak?
5 What language does he speak at work? Is this a problem for him?

English at work

What do these people have in common – a banker in Mexico City, a waiter in a five-star hotel in Moscow, and a worker in the Hitachi electronics factory in Tokyo? They all speak English at work. Today, English is the common language in multinational companies in countries from France to Singapore.

Jean-Paul Piat works for an IT company in Paris. Every day he has meetings with other managers in English. He also reads documents and writes e-mails in English, and speaks on the phone in English to offices in other countries.

"We're a multinational company with offices all over the world," says Jean-Paul. "We also have some people in our Paris office who aren't French. We need a common language to communicate, and that language is English. I think it is a good idea, but some people don't like speaking English in a meeting when nearly everybody is French."

c Look at the highlighted words and phrases. Guess their meaning. Check with your teacher or a dictionary.

d Is English important for <u>your</u> job?

WORDS AND PHRASES TO LEARN
What do you do?
I'm a *doctor*.
Where do you work?
I work *in a hospital*.
I like it very much.
He speaks *English* very well.
only
speak on the phone
all over the world

What time is it?
It's six thirty.

What time is it?

1 TELLING TIME

a **3.25** Listen and match the dialogues and pictures.

> **1 A** What time is it?
> **B** It's six thirty. Go back to sleep.
> **A** OK. Have a nice day.
> **B** You, too.
>
> **2 A** Excuse me. What time is it?
> **B** Sorry, I don't know. I don't have a watch.
>
> **A** Excuse me. What time is it?
> **C** Just a moment. It's quarter to seven.
> **A** Thanks.
> **C** You're welcome.

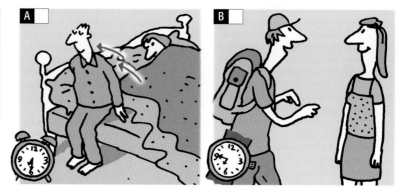

b **3.26** Listen and repeat the dialogues in **a**. Practice with a partner.

c ⊙ **p.110 Vocabulary Bank** *The time and ordinal numbers*. Do part **A**.

d **3.28** Listen and draw the time on the clocks.

1 2 3 4 5 6 7 8

e Practice with a partner.

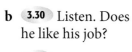
Number 1. What time is it?

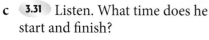
It's nine o'clock.

f ⊙ **Communication** *What time is it?* A p.77 B p.79.

2 PEOPLE ON THE STREET 📺

> 1 What do you do?
> 2 Do you like it?
> 3 What time do you start and finish?

a **3.29** Listen to Christian. What does he do?

He's a / an _____.

Christian

b **3.30** Listen. Does he like his job?

c **3.31** Listen. What time does he start and finish?

He starts work at _____.
He finishes work at _____.

d **3.32** Listen to four more people and complete the chart.

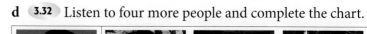

	Megan	Pamela	Chris	Daniel
Job?				
Likes it? ✔ ✗				
Starts / finishes?	_____ / _____	_____ / _____	_____ / _____	_____ / _____

e In pairs, ask and answer the questions in the box.

3 VOCABULARY days of the week

a **3.33** Listen and repeat the days of the week. Practice saying them.

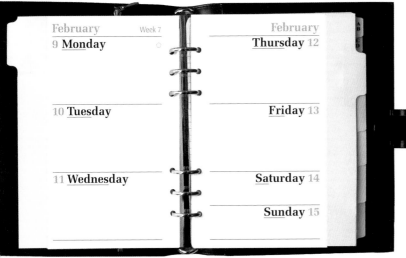

February	Week 7	February
9 **Monday**		**Thursday** 12
10 **Tuesday**		**Friday** 13
11 **Wednesday**		**Saturday** 14
		Sunday 15

⚠ Days of the week begin with a CAPITAL letter, e.g., Monday NOT ~~monday~~

b **3.34** Listen and complete the dialogues with days of the week. Practice the dialogues with a partner.

1
Man What day is it today?
Woman It's ¹ _____. Why?
Man Because it's my wife's birthday on ² _____, and I don't have a present!

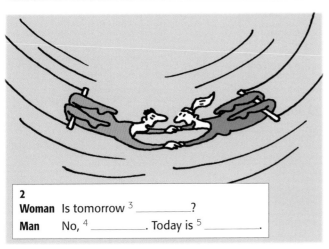

2
Woman Is tomorrow ³ _____?
Man No, ⁴ _____. Today is ⁵ _____.

c **3.35** Listen and repeat. Practice saying good-bye with different days of the week.

Saying good-bye

Good-bye. / See you on (Monday).

Bye. / See you tomorrow.

d Ask and answer with a partner.

What day is it today?
What day is it tomorrow?
What day(s) do you have English classes?
What's your favorite day of the week?

4 PRONUNCIATION silent consonants

a **3.36** Listen and repeat the words. Practice saying them.

answer	Wednesday	know	listen
white	school	talk	write

b **3.37** Listen. Practice the sentences.

Don't write on the whiteboard.
I don't know the school.
Talk to you on Wednesday.

5 **3.38** SONG ♫ *Friday I'm in love*

WORDS AND PHRASES TO LEARN

What time is it?
Have a nice day.
 You, too.
Thanks.
 You're welcome.
What day is it today?
What day is it tomorrow?
Why?
 Because it's *my wife's* birthday.
See you on *Monday.*

GRAMMAR

Circle the correct answer.

Hello, _____ Alex.
a I   (b) I'm

1 _____ you want a coffee?
a Are   b Do

2 _____ dogs?
a Like you   b Do you like

3 I _____ fast food.
a don't eat   b not eat

4 A Do you live downtown?
B Yes, I _____.
a do   b live

5 In Japan, we _____ rice for breakfast.
a have   b has

6 Jack _____ in a language school.
a work   b works

7 _____ she speak English?
a Do   b Does

8 He _____ Spanish at a university.
a teachs   b teaches

9 My brother _____ children.
a doesn't have   b don't have

10 A What does Gavin _____?
B He's a doctor.
a work   b do

VOCABULARY

a Write the verb.

_____watch_____ TV

1 _____ to the radio

2 _____ English

3 _____ in an apartment

4 _____ the newspaper

5 _____ breakfast

b Circle the different word.

(soda)   meat   fish

1 breakfast   lunch   bread

2 Monday   Wednesday   twenty

3 hospital   waiter   office

4 fruit   coffee   water

5 nurse   bank   lawyer

c Write the times.

_____ quarter past seven _____

1 _____

2 _____

3 _____

4 _____

5 _____

d Complete the phrases.

A What d**ay** is it today?   B Friday.

1 A What t_____ is it?   B It's five thirty.

2 A What do you have for breakfast?   B It d_____.

3 A What's her phone number?   B Sorry. I don't **kn**_____

4 A Do you want some water?   B Yes, p_____.

5 A Do you drink a **l**_____ of coffee?   B Yes, six cups a day!

PRONUNCIATION

a Can you remember these words and sounds?

vowels   consonants

b ⊙ **p.117 / 119 Sound Bank.** Check the words and sounds, and practice saying the example words.

c Underline the stressed syllable.
Italian

breakfast   potatoes   assistant   policeman   Saturday

1 CAN YOU UNDERSTAND THIS TEXT?

a Read the text and complete it with food words from the list.

sausage butter fish fruit meat salads

Eat the Mediterranean way

Doctors say that the traditional diet in some Mediterranean countries, for example Greece and Italy, is very healthy.

Why is it good for you?
In these countries, people eat a lot of ¹ _____ and vegetables, bread, pasta, rice, fish, and olive oil. They don't eat a lot of red ² _____ or butter. This diet is very good for your heart, and people in these countries live longer than in other countries.

How to eat like Mediterranean people and live a long life:

- Eat a lot of fruit and vegetables every day.
- Use olive oil for cooking and for ³ _____.
- Don't eat ⁴ _____ with your bread.
- Eat a lot of ⁵ _____. Don't eat a lot of meat, for example, ⁶ _____.
- Sit down with your family for lunch and dinner. Don't hurry your meals!

b Do you eat "the Mediterranean way"?

2 CAN YOU WRITE THIS IN ENGLISH?

a Read the two texts. Complete the sentences with *Min-ji* or *Woo-jin*.

1 _____ has a job.
2 _____ has a girlfriend / boyfriend.
3 _____ doesn't live with his / her family.
4 _____ lives downtown.
5 _____ studies a language.

My sister
My sister's name is Min-ji. She's 26 years old, and she's a nurse. She works in a big hospital in Incheon. She lives in an apartment in Bucheon, about 12 km from Incheon. She lives with two friends. They are nurses, too. She doesn't have a boyfriend, but she has a lot of friends.

My friend Woo-jin
My friend Woo-jin is a student at Inha University in Incheon. He studies English. He wants to be a teacher. He lives with his family in an apartment downtown in Incheon. He has a girlfriend, and her name is Ji-hyun. She's very nice too.

b Write about two people: a member of your family and a friend.

3 CAN YOU UNDERSTAND THESE PEOPLE?

3.39 Listen and complete the form.

Marshall Language School Student Registration	
First name	
Last name	
Nationality	
Age	
Occupation	
Brothers / Sisters at school No ☐ Yes ☐	
Name _____ Class number _____	
Phone number _____	

4 CAN YOU SAY THIS IN ENGLISH?

Check (✔) the boxes.
Can you...?

say where you live and what you do	☐ Yes, I can.
ask where other people live and what they do	☐ Yes, I can.
say what you have for breakfast	☐ Yes, I can.
say what people eat in your country	☐ Yes, I can.
ask and say what time it is	☐ Yes, I can.
say the days of the week	☐ Yes, I can.

G adverbs of frequency, simple present
V a typical day
P sentence stress

What time do you get up?
I usually get up at 7:30.

Do you like mornings?

1 LISTENING & SPEAKING

a Read the questionnaire and write your answers.

Do you like mornings?

1 What time do you get up?
2 Do you take a shower?
3 What do you have for breakfast?
4 Do you have breakfast sitting down or standing up?
5 What time do you go to work? (school)
6 Are you in a hurry in the morning?
7 Do you like mornings?

b **4.1** Anna Kenyon is 29. She works for a music company. Listen and write her answers.

c **4.2** Listen and repeat questions 1–7.

d Ask your partner the questions.

2 VOCABULARY A typical day

a ⊙ **p.111 Vocabulary Bank** *A typical day*.

b Can you remember? Mime or draw five verb phrases for your partner to guess.

3 PRONUNCIATION sentence stress

a **4.5** Listen and repeat. Copy the rhythm.

<u>What</u> <u>time</u> do you <u>get</u> <u>up</u>?
At <u>seven</u> o'clock.
<u>What</u> <u>time</u> do you have <u>breakfast</u>?
At <u>seven</u> <u>thirty</u>.
<u>What</u> <u>time</u> do you <u>go</u> to <u>work</u>?
At <u>eight</u> o'clock.

b Ask and answer the questions with a partner.

What time do you…?
get up	go home
have breakfast	have dinner
have lunch	go to bed

4 GRAMMAR adverbs of frequency

a Match sentences 1–4 with a–d.

	M	T	W	Th	F
1 I **always** get up at 7:30… ☐	✔	✔	✔	✔	✔
2 I **never** drink coffee… ☐	✘	✘	✘	✘	✘
3 I **usually** finish work at 5:00… ☐	✔	✔	✘	✔	✔
4 I **sometimes** watch a movie on TV… ☐	✘	✔	✘	✘	✔

a but on Wednesdays I finish at 7:00.
b or I read and listen to music.
c because I start work at 8:30.
d because I don't like it.

b ⊙ **p.94 Grammar Bank 4A.** Read the rules and do the exercises.

c In pairs, make true sentences about <u>you</u>. Use *always, usually, sometimes,* or *never*.

listen to the radio in the car
read a newspaper in the morning
drink black coffee
make dinner
have meat for lunch
watch movies on my computer
go to the gym
do housework in the evening

I never listen to the radio in the car. I listen to CDs.

5 READING

a Read the article. Use the glossary to help you and answer the questions in pairs.

A day in the life of James Blunt

James Blunt is an ex-soldier who is now a singer. He lives alone in Ibiza, Spain.

 I live in a beautiful old house. It's about 150 years old, and it's on a hill with a lot of trees. From my window, I have a fantastic view of the ocean.

I usually get up at about 9:30, and I take a shower. I always wear jeans and a T-shirt. Clothes don't really interest me. I have two pairs of jeans, one jacket, and six T-shirts. I never have breakfast – I'm not hungry in the morning. I make a fire and clean the house. Then I play the piano, or I sit on the sofa and play the guitar.

I live near a small village. For lunch, I go and buy bread and a can of tuna, or maybe ham or cheese. I never cook. After lunch, I sometimes work in the garden. I don't have a TV – I only have a music system and my music collection. I like singer-songwriters from the 1970s, like Lou Reed and Leonard Cohen.

In the evening, I usually go out with friends. We have dinner at one of the old Spanish bars, and then we sometimes go to a club. Before I go to bed, I lock the doors. When I'm in bed, I look out of the window at the night sky and think how wonderful life is.

Glossary

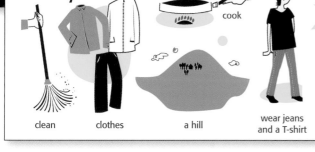

clean   clothes   a hill   wear jeans and a T-shirt

play the guitar   buy bread   lock   a fire

1 Where does James live?
2 What time does he get up?
3 What clothes does he wear?
4 Does he have breakfast?
5 What does he do in the morning?
6 What does he have for lunch?
7 What does he do after lunch?
8 Does he watch TV?
9 What does he do in the evening?

b Look at the highlighted "time" words and guess their meaning. Check with your teacher or a dictionary.

c Complete the sentences with a highlighted word from the text.

1 I get up at 7:00. _____ I have breakfast.
2 _____ I go out in the evening, I usually go to a club.
3 I never drink coffee _____ dinner.
4 I always take a shower _____ I go to bed.
5 On the weekend, I go to bed at _____ eleven thirty.

d Do you think James Blunt's day is typical for a pop singer? Why (not)?

6 SPEAKING & WRITING

a ● p.111 **Vocabulary Bank** *A typical day.* Write about your typical morning. Use adverbs of frequency (*always*, *usually*, etc.) and time words (*then*, *after breakfast*, etc.).

b Tell a partner about <u>your</u> typical afternoon and evening.

> I usually have lunch at two o'clock.
> I have a sandwich or a salad.

WORDS AND PHRASES TO LEARN

What time do you *get up*?
   At *eight o'clock*.
He gets up at about *9:30*.
wear *jeans*
clean
in the morning / afternoon / evening
before / after *lunch*
then
go out
a club
lock the doors
When I'm in bed…

4

B

G word order in questions; question words
V common verbs 2
P /ɛr/, /ɑ/, /aʊ/, and /y/

Do you play sports?
What sports do you play?

Life at the top of the world

1 READING

a Look at the photos. Do you prefer Hammerfest in the winter or in the summer?

b Read the introduction about Hammerfest and answer the questions.

1 Where is Hammerfest?
2 How is life different in the winter and in the summer?

c Now read the interview with Knut-Arne Iversen. Match the questions with his answers.

☐ Do you like life in Hammerfest?

☐ Do you prefer the summer or the winter?

☐ Is the winter very cold?

1 Do a lot of tourists come to Hammerfest?

☐ What do people do in the summer?

☐ What do people do in the winter?

☐ When do they usually come?

d **4.7** Listen and check.

e Read the interview again. Then match the highlighted words with their opposites.

1 cold _____
2 easy _____
3 light _____
4 long _____
5 outside _____
6 summer _____
7 the same _____
8 open _____

f Ask and answer the questions in **c** about your town / city.

Hammerfest is a small town in the north of Norway. It is near the Arctic Circle. Only 9,407 people live here. In the winter, it is light for only two or three hours. People have breakfast, lunch, and dinner in the dark. In the summer, it is light for 24 hours, and people go to bed very late. Some people play golf in the midnight sun!

2 GRAMMAR   word order in questions

a Re-order the words to make questions. Then answer them from memory.

Knut-Arne from where is _____ ?

Norway in Hammerfest is _____ ?

does Knut-Arne work where _____ ?

in do ocean the people swim _____ ?

b ▶ **p.94 Grammar Bank 4B.** Read the rules and do the exercises.

36

INTERVIEW

KNUT-ARNE IVERSEN is from Hammerfest. He works for the Tourist Information Office.

1 *Do a lot of tourists come to Hammerfest?*
Yes, about 175,000 a year.

2
In the summer. We don't have a lot of tourists in the winter!

3
No, not very, about −3 degrees [°C]. But we sometimes have a lot of snow, and the streets and schools are closed.

4
We play a lot of sports. We ski a lot, and we have snowmobiles. Children usually play outside, but if it's very cold, they play inside on their computer or watch TV. In the evening, we usually stay at home and relax or go and see friends. But the winter is difficult for old people.

5
Life is completely different. It's light for 24 hours a day, and the weather is sometimes very hot. People are outside all the time. We fish, and walk, and have barbecues. We don't swim because the water is very cold – maybe only 10 degrees [°C]. People don't sleep a lot, and young children say, "I don't want to go to bed. It isn't dark."

6
In the winter, it's nice to be at home with your family and friends, but I prefer the summer.

7
Yes. Life here is easy. It's quiet and beautiful, and the air is clean. But the winter is very long, and the summer is very short. I'm not sure if I will stay here forever.

3 VOCABULARY common verbs 2

a Can you remember? Complete the phrases with a verb from the list.

do	eat	go (x2)	have	listen	read	watch

1 I _____ shopping. 5 I _____ housework.
2 I _____ TV. 6 I _____ to the gym.
3 I _____ magazines. 7 I _____ dinner.
4 I _____ to the radio. 8 I _____ fast food.

b ⟶ **p.112 Vocabulary Bank** *Common verbs 2*. Do part **A**.

4 PRONUNCIATION /ɛr/, /ɑ/, /aʊ/, and /y/

a **4.10** Listen and repeat the words and sounds.

ɛ	where	there	their	hairdresser
ɑ	what	watch	hot	shopping
aʊ	how	town	mountains	outside
y	you	yes	usually	music	computer

b **4.11** Listen and say the sentences. Copy the sounds and rhythm.

Where do you live? Over there.
What TV shows do you watch?
What music do you usually listen to?
How do you relax? I walk in the mountains.

5 SPEAKING

In pairs, ask and answer the questions.

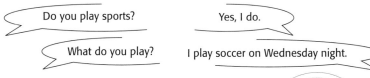

Do you play sports?   Yes, I do.

What do you play?   I play soccer on Wednesday night.

YOUR LIFE

During the week
/ play sports? What / play?
/ listen to music? What music / listen to?
/ watch TV? What shows / watch?

On the weekend
/ go out on Friday or Saturday night? What / do?
/ go shopping? Where / go shopping?
/ walk or play sports? What / play?
/ go to the beach or the mountains? Where / go?
/ read a newspaper on Sunday? What paper / read?
Where / usually have lunch on Sunday?
How / relax on Sunday evening?

⚠ **at** night / ten o'clock
on Saturday (morning / afternoon / the weekend)
in the summer / winter

WORDS AND PHRASES TO LEARN

the north	outside / inside
It's hot. / It's cold.	the same / different
the summer / the winter	snow
open / closed	relax
light / dark	
ocean	

4 C

G *can / can't*: permission and possibility
V common verbs 2
P sentence rhythm

> Can I park here?
> No, you can't. You can park in the parking lot.

You can't park here

1 GRAMMAR *can / can't*: permission and possibility

a `4.12` Cover the dialogues and look at the pictures. What do you think the people are saying? Listen and check.

1

Policeman	Excuse me. You can't park there.
Woman	No? Why not?
Policeman	The sign says, "no parking."
Woman	Oh, I'm sorry, officer. Where can I park near here?
Policeman	You can park over there, ma'am, in the parking lot.
Woman	Thank you, officer.

2

Ellie	Hi, Matt.
Matt	Hi. Who's this?
Ellie	It's me, Ellie. How are you?
Matt	Oh, fine, thanks.
Ellie	Matt, can you come to dinner on Friday?
Matt	On Friday? Oh, I'm really sorry. I can't come. It's my girlfriend's birthday.
Ellie	Your girlfriend?
Matt	Yes, Lucy, from work.
Ellie	Oh. Lucy.
Matt	Sorry about dinner.
Ellie	That's OK. Bye.

b Listen again and read the dialogues. Answer the questions.

1 Why does the policeman speak to the woman?
2 Where does the woman park at the end of the conversation?
3 Is the policeman angry ☹ with her?

4 What's Ellie's plan for Friday?
5 Does Matt say yes or no to Ellie? Why?
6 Is Ellie happy ☺ or sad ☹ at the end of the conversation?

c Look at the highlighted phrases. Which dialogue is about a possibility? Which dialogue is about permission to do something?

d ⟳ **p.94 Grammar Bank 4C.** Read the rules and do the exercises.

2 PRONUNCIATION
sentence rhythm

a `4.14` Listen and repeat the sounds and sentences. Copy the rhythm.

 Can I park here?
Yes, you can.
No, you can't.
You can't park here.

 Where can I park?
You can park here.

b `4.15` Listen. Can you hear the difference?

1 a We can park here.
  b We can't park here.

2 a I can help you.
  b I can't help you.

3 a We can stop here.
  b We can't stop here.

4 a You can sit here.
  b You can't sit here.

5 a Mark can go with me.
  b Mark can't go with me.

6 a I can walk home.
  b I can't walk home.

7 a We can come tonight.
  b We can't come tonight.

8 a You can write in the book.
  b You can't write in the book.

c `4.16` Listen. Circle a or b.

d Practice the dialogues in exercise **1a** with a partner.

3 VOCABULARY common verbs 2

a What do these signs mean? Explain with *You can... / You can't...*

b ○ **p.112 Vocabulary Bank** *Common verbs 2*. Do part **B**.

c In pairs, complete the sentences with a verb.

1 You can't _____ here.

2 You can _____ money here.

3 You can't _____ your cell phone here.

4 You can _____ by credit card here.

5 You can't _____ photos here.

6 You can _____ the Internet here.

7 You can't _____ fast here.

8 You can't _____ soccer here.

d Cover the sentences and look at the signs. Say what they mean.

4 SPEAKING & WRITING

a Answer the questions with a partner.

In your town / city
can you...?

- pay by credit card in small stores
- drive and talk on a cell phone
- drive fast downtown
- take photos in museums
- go shopping on Sundays
- park on the street without paying

At work
can you...?

- start and finish work when you want
- send personal e-mails
- take a break when you want

At school
can you...?

- come into class if you're late
- go home for lunch
- use the Internet
- use your cell phone

b Write two things you can do and two you can't do
i) in your town / city and ii) at work / school.

In Boston, you can pay by credit card in small stores, and....

You can't...

At work, I can...

WORDS AND PHRASES TO LEARN
I'm (really) sorry.
That's OK.
Who's this?
It's me.
sir
ma'am

4
PRACTICAL ENGLISH

Saying and understanding prices
Buying a coffee
/ʊr/, /s/, and /k/

How much is it?

Can I have an espresso, please?
How much is it?

1 UNDERSTANDING PRICES

a **4.18** Listen and repeat.

twenty **euros**

fifty **cents**

twenty **dollars**

twenty-five **cents**

twenty **pounds**

fifty **pence** (fifty **p**)

b Match the prices and words.

1	£12.75	☐
2	$15.99	☐
3	€50.99	☐
4	£120	☐
5	$13.25	☐
6	€3.20	☐
7	60p	☐
8	$0.80	☐

A   a hundred and twenty pounds
B   eighty cents
C   fifteen dollars and ninety-nine cents
D   fifty euros ninety-nine
E   sixty p
F   thirteen dollars and twenty-five cents
G   three euros twenty
H   twelve pounds seventy-five

c **4.19** Listen and check. Then listen and repeat.

d Cover the words and look at the prices. Practice saying them.

e **4.20** Listen to four conversations. How much is it?
Circle the right price.

1

$1.25 $1.35

2

£15   £50

3

$4.99 $9.49

4

€30.20   €13.20

f ➡ **p.84.** Listen again with the audioscript.

2 PRONUNCIATION /ʊr/, /s/, and /k/

a **4.21** Listen and repeat the words and sounds.

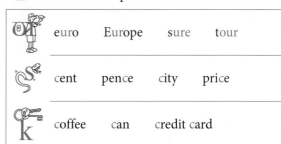

ʊr	euro	Europe	sure	tour
s	cent	pence	city	price
k	coffee	can	credit card	

b **4.22** Listen. Practice the sentences.

In Europe, a lot of countries use the euro.
The ticket is six euros and sixty cents.
Can I have a cup of coffee, please?

3 BUYING A COFFEE

a 4.23 Read the menu and listen. What does the woman ask for? How much is it?

Espresso	Single 1.25	Double 1.40	Chocolate Brownie	1.20
Americano	Regular 1.55	Large 1.75	Muffin	1.35
Cappuccino	Regular 1.75	Large 1.90	Cookies	1.25
Latte	Regular 1.75	Large 1.90		
Tea	Regular 1.25	Large 1.50		

Cafe Noir

b Listen again and read the dialogue. Write the missing words.

c 4.24 Listen and repeat. Practice the dialogue with a partner.

> Use *Can I have…, please?* to ask for things in a cafe, a store, etc.

d Practice with a partner. Ask the prices on the menu.

> How much is a regular latte? $1.75.

Waiter	Can I help you?
Woman	Yes, can I have a ¹ _____ and a chocolate brownie, please?
Waiter	Espresso, Americano, or cappuccino?
Woman	An espresso, ² _____.
Waiter	Single or ³ _____?
Woman	Single. ⁴ _____ much is it?
Waiter	Two dollars and forty-five cents.
Woman	⁵ _____ you are.
Waiter	Thanks.

e Role-play the conversation in **b**. **A** you are the waiter / waitress, **B** you are the customer. Ask for <u>two</u> things. Then change roles.

A
> Can I help you?

B
> Can I have a regular latte and a muffin, please?

4 PEOPLE ON THE STREET

> 1 Where do you usually have lunch?
> 2 What do you have?
> 3 How much is it?

a 4.25 Listen to Brandy. Where does she usually have lunch?

Brandy

b 4.26 Listen. What does she have?

c 4.27 Listen. How much is it?

d 4.28 Listen to four more people and complete the chart.

e In pairs, ask and answer the questions in the box.

5 4.29 SONG ♫ *Money, money, money*

	Bridget	Michael	Helen	Dax
Place				
Food				
Price	£	About $	About £	About $

WORDS AND PHRASES TO LEARN

Can I help you?

Can I have *an espresso*, please?
  Single or double?

How much is it?

Can I pay with *MasterCard*™?
  Sure.

A ticket to *Paris*, please.
  One-way or round trip?

Here you are.

a memory card

a phone card

4   What do you remember?

GRAMMAR

Circle the correct answer.

Hello, ____ Alex.
a I   (b) I'm

1 I ____ cereal for breakfast.
  a usually have   b have usually
2 She ____ to bed before 12:00.
  a doesn't never go   b never goes
3 What ____ in the summer?
  a do people do   b do people
4 ____ your phone?
  a This is   b Is this
5 **A** ____ do you listen to music?
  B In the morning.
  a Where   b When
6 **A** ____ soccer?
  B No, he prefers tennis.
  a Does he like   b Does like he
7 ____ park here?
  a Can I   b Do I can
8 You ____ use your cell phone here.
  a can't   b ca'nt
9 **A** Can they come on Friday?
  B Yes, they ____.
  a do   b can
10 John ____ sit here.
  a can   b cans

VOCABULARY

a Complete with a word from the list.

gym   home   breakfast   shower   work   ~~up~~

get *up*

1 have ____
2 take a ____
3 go to ____
4 go ____
5 go to the ____

b Complete with a common verb.

On the weekend, we sometimes *walk* in the mountains.

1 I always ____ to the movies on Saturday.
2 Can I ____ by credit card?
3 You can't ____ photos in this museum.
4 Do you ____ sports?
5 Don't ____ by a "no parking" sign.

c Complete with a preposition from the list.

~~on~~   at   for   in   in   on

What do you usually do *on* the weekend?
1 We go to the beach ____ the summer.
2 I usually have lunch ____ 2:30.
3 Can you come to dinner ____ Friday?
4 What do you usually have ____ breakfast?
5 I always watch TV ____ the evening.

d Write the prices.

£1.50   *one pound fifty*
1 $20 ____
2 €8.25 ____
3 £9.99 ____
4 $0.70 ____
5 80p ____

e Complete the phrases.

Do you **p**refer tea or coffee?
1 **A** How **m**____ is that?
  B It's $4.50.
2 **A** I'm sorry.
  B T____ OK.
3 **A** Can I **h**____ an espresso, please?
  B Here you are.
4 **A** Is the exercise easy?
  B No, it's very **d**____.
5 **A** A ticket to Los Angeles, please.
  B One-way or **r**____ trip?

PRONUNCIATION

a Can you remember these words and sounds?

vowels

consonants

b ➲ **p.117 / 119 Sound Bank.** Check the words and sounds, and practice saying the example words.

c Underline the stressed syllable.

Italian

piano   housework   dollar   before   sometimes

1 CAN YOU UNDERSTAND THIS TEXT?

a Read the article and mark the sentences T (true) or F (false).

1 American people always have breakfast at home.
2 They usually work 35–40 hours a week.
3 They have lunch from 1:00–2:30.
4 A lot of people have lunch at home.
5 They usually have dinner at 5:30.
6 A lot of people go to bed after midnight.
7 You can go shopping every day in the US.
8 Big supermarkets in the US close on Sunday.

Meal times and business hours in the US

In the US, people usually start work between 8:00 and 9:00 a.m. Some people have breakfast at home, but a lot of people just buy a coffee and something to eat when they go to work.

Most people work five days a week. The typical working day is seven or eight hours with a short lunch (half an hour to an hour) at about 12:00 p.m. People don't go home for lunch – they just have a sandwich in a cafe or in their office. People usually finish work at 5:00 or 6:00. They have dinner between 6:00 and 7:00, and this is usually the big meal of the day. During the week, they usually go to bed between 10:00 and 11:30 p.m.

People go shopping after work or on the weekend. Some stores close early during the week (5:30–6:00 p.m.), but supermarkets and a lot of stores are open until 8:00 in the evening or later. Some stores are also open on Sunday, and big supermarkets are open 24 hours a day, seven days a week.

b Look at the highlighted time phrases and guess their meaning. Check with your teacher or a dictionary.

c Compare the information in the text with your country. What is the same? What is different?

2 CAN YOU WRITE THIS IN ENGLISH?

a Read the text. Is your typical Sunday similar to Larissa's?

Larissa Silva is a teacher. She lives in Brasília.

My typical Sunday

On Sunday, I usually get up late, at about ten o'clock. I go to a cafe for breakfast. I always have a cappuccino and a chocolate croissant, and I read the Sunday newspapers. Then I usually meet my friends. We go shopping, or we walk in the park. We have lunch in a restaurant. After lunch, we talk, relax, and drink coffee. We go home at about five thirty. In the evening, I prepare for my classes, and then I have dinner and watch TV. I go to bed early, and I think about next weekend.

b Write about your typical Saturday or Sunday.

3 CAN YOU UNDERSTAND THESE PEOPLE?

4.30 Listen and choose the right answer.

1 What time does Jack get up?
   a 6:45. b 7:15.
2 What does Carol usually have for breakfast?
   a Sausage and eggs. b Cereal and fruit.
3 What time does Martin finish work on Friday?
   a 5:00. b 6:00.
4 When does Julia usually go shopping?
   a On Saturday. b On Sunday.
5 Where does the man park?
   a In the parking lot. b On the street.
6 What languages does the woman speak?
   a Spanish. b Spanish and Italian.
7 What does the woman buy?
   a A cappuccino and two brownies.
   b Two cappuccinos and a brownie.
8 How much is the pen?
   a $2.60. b $2.70.

4 CAN YOU SAY THIS IN ENGLISH?

Check (✔) the boxes.
Can you…?

say what you do on a typical day	☐ Yes, I can.
ask about other people's days	☐ Yes, I can.
say what people can / can't do in your country	☐ Yes, I can.
ask for things in a cafe or store	☐ Yes, I can.
ask about prices	☐ Yes, I can.

G simple past: *be*
V *in, at, on*: places
P /ər/ and *was / were*

> Where were you? I was at the movies.

Before they were famous...

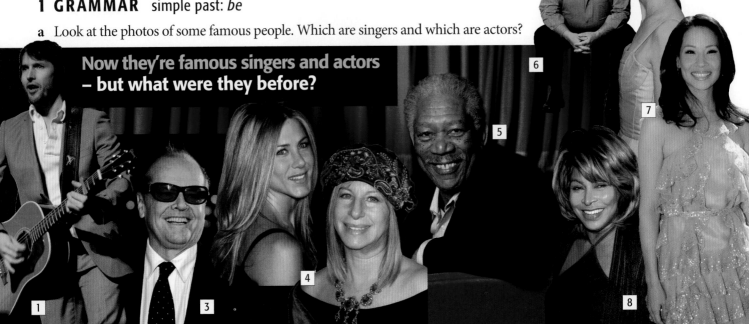

Now they're famous singers and actors – but what were they before?

1 GRAMMAR simple past: *be*

a Look at the photos of some famous people. Which are singers and which are actors?

b Can you guess their old jobs? Choose from the jobs below.

aerobics teacher	English teacher	hairdresser
nurse waitress soldier mechanic salesperson		

1 James Blunt was a _____.
2 Sting was an _____.
3 Jack Nicholson was a _____.
4 Jennifer Aniston and Barbra Streisand were _____.
5 Morgan Freeman was a _____.
6 Danny DeVito was a _____.
7 Lucy Liu and Calista Flockhart were _____.
8 Tina Turner was a _____.

c **5.1** Listen and check.

d Complete the chart.

Present	Past
Sting **is** a singer.	He _____ a teacher.
They **are** actors.	They _____ aerobics teachers.

e ○ **p.96 Grammar Bank 5A.** Read the rules and do the exercises.

2 PRONUNCIATION /ər/ and *was / were*

a **5.3** Listen and repeat the words and sound.

nurse	work	her	word	first

b **5.4** Listen and repeat the sounds and sentences. Copy the <u>rhythm</u>.

<u>Were</u> they <u>famous</u>?
<u>Yes</u>, they <u>were</u>.
<u>No</u>, they <u>weren't</u>. They <u>weren't</u> <u>famous</u>.

<u>Was</u> she a <u>teacher</u>?
<u>Yes</u>, she <u>was</u>.
<u>No</u>, she <u>wasn't</u>. She <u>wasn't</u> a <u>teacher</u>.

c **5.5** Listen and say the sentences in the past.
"*He's a teacher.*"

> He was a teacher.

3 VOCABULARY *in, at, on*: places

a Can you remember? Complete with *in*, *at*, or *on*.

1 Here's your key. You're _____ room 210.
2 I'm a writer. I work _____ home.
3 My wife isn't here. She's _____ work.
4 Where's my coat? Oh, no! It's _____ the train.

b **5.6** Complete the chart with *in*, *at*, or *on*. Listen and check. Repeat the phrases.

1 _____	2 _____	3 _____
home	bed	a bus
work	the bedroom	a train
school	a car	a plane
the gym	Chicago	the street
the airport	a meeting	
the theater	the park	
a restaurant		
the hairdresser		

c Test a partner. **A** (book open) say a place. **B** (book closed) say the phrase. Then change roles.

A
> bedroom

B
> in the bedroom

d **5.7** Where was Mike yesterday? Listen and complete the sentences.

1 At 6:00 ___*he was in bed*___ .
2 At 7:00 _____ .
3 At 8:00 _____ .
4 At 10:00 _____ .
5 At 12:00 _____ .
6 At 2:00 _____ .
7 At 6:00 _____ .
8 At 7:00 _____ .
9 At 8:00 _____ .
10 At 10:00 _____ again!

4 SPEAKING

a Look at the pictures for two minutes. Try to remember who the people are and where they were yesterday at three o'clock.

b ◯ **Communication** *Where were they? A p.77 B p.80.*

c In pairs, ask and answer.

Where were you yesterday at 6:30 / 10:00 in the morning?
Where were you yesterday at 3:15 / 5:30 in the afternoon?
Where were you at 9:00 / 11:00 last night?
Where were you last Friday / Saturday night?

> Where were you yesterday at 6:30 in the morning?

WORDS AND PHRASES TO LEARN
yesterday
yesterday afternoon
last night
last Saturday

5
B

G simple past: *have, go, get*
V irregular verbs; review of daily routine verbs
P sentence stress

> Did you have a good day?
> Yes, I had a great day.

A perfect day?

1 VOCABULARY review of daily routine verbs

Can you remember? ◯ **p.111 Vocabulary Bank** *A typical day.* Test a partner.

> **A** Picture 8?
>
> **B** They have lunch at two o'clock. Picture 13?

2 LISTENING

a **5.8** Ben is in Paris on business. His 17-year-old daughter, Linda, is at home in Toronto. Listen and check (✔) the places where she was during the day.

☐ at school
☐ at the gym
☐ at a museum
☐ at the hairdresser
☐ at a cafe
☐ at a restaurant
☐ at a shopping mall
☐ at the movies

b Listen again and complete the dialogue.

Linda Hello.
Ben Hi, honey.
Linda Oh, hi, Dad. How's Paris?
Ben Fine. A lot of work. Did you have a good ¹ **d**_____?
Linda It was OK.
Ben What did you do?
Linda I got ² **u**_____ early. I went to school.
Ben How was it?
Linda ³ **G**_____! We didn't have classes. We went to an ⁴ **a**_____ museum.
Ben Oh, nice. Did you have ⁵ **l**_____ there?
Linda Yes, we had lunch at the cafe. And then I went ⁶ **s**_____ with Katy.
Ben Did you do your homework?
Linda Yes, of course. I ⁷ **a**_____ do my homework.
Ben Who's that, Linda?

c **5.9** Listen to the end of the conversation and answer the questions.

1 Where is Linda's mother?
2 Who is Linda with?

3 GRAMMAR simple past: *have, go, get*

a Read the dialogue in **2b** again and complete the chart.

Present	Past
What do you do?	What _____ you do?
I get up early.	I _____ up early.
We don't have classes.	We _____ have classes.
We go to an art museum.	We _____ to an art museum.
We have lunch at the cafe.	We _____ lunch at the cafe.

b **5.10** Listen and check. Then repeat the present and past sentences.

c ◯ **p.96 Grammar Bank 5B.** Read the rules and do the exercises.

4 PRONUNCIATION & SPEAKING sentence stress

a **5.12** Listen to the questions in the chart. What two words are missing? Are the missing words stressed?

YESTERDAY	YOUR PARTNER
1 What time / get up?	
2 / have breakfast? What / have?	
3 / go to work (school)?	
4 Where / have lunch? What / have?	
5 / go to the gym?	
6 / go shopping?	
7 / have dinner at home? What / have?	
8 / watch TV? What / watch?	
9 What time / go to bed?	

b Listen again and repeat the questions.

c Interview your partner about yesterday. Write his / her information in the chart.

5 READING & WRITING

a Read the introduction to the article. What did a lot of people do on March 20, 2009?

A ☐ B ☐ C ☐ D ☐ E ☐ F ☐

A DAY
IN THE LIFE...

20 MARCH 2009

On March 20, 2009, a lot of people in the US wrote blogs about what they did the day before. The idea was to give a picture of life at the beginning of the 21st century.

1 Casey, from Michigan

Yesterday was the first day of spring, but there was snow on my car in the morning! Brrr…not a very warm spring day! I didn't have students today, but I went to work because I had a lot of paperwork. I had lesson plans, too. Later, I had dinner with my family at home, and after that, there was a basketball game on TV—the Detroit Pistons and the LA Clippers!

2 Mariah, New York

7:00 a.m.	I got up.
7:30 a.m.	I went for a walk with my dog in the park. It was a beautiful spring morning.
9:00 a.m.	I went to work on the subway. I had a difficult day in the office. I was very stressed.
12:30 p.m.	I went to SoHo for lunch.
6:30 p.m.	I went home.
7:00 p.m.	I went to the park again with my dog.
8:00 p.m.	I had dinner at home—pasta and salad.
11:30 p.m.	I went to bed.

3 Jared, from Arizona

A day in the life of a stay-at-home dad! It was the usual— breakfast, housework, and diapers! Then my daughter had a nap for two hours. It was a wonderful surprise! I had a long lunch and did some work. In the afternoon, we went to the park, and then we went shopping. At night, we had a babysitter, and my wife and I went to a pizza restaurant with friends.

Glossary
lesson plans notes for teaching a class
SoHo an area of New York City with a lot of restaurants
a stay-at-home dad a father who stays at home with the children
diapers things babies wear under clothes
have a nap sleep for a short time

---

b Now read three people's blogs. Use the glossary to help you. Match two photos to each blog.

c Read the blogs again. Complete the sentences with C (Casey), M (Mariah), or J (Jared).

1 ___ has a child
2 ___ is a teacher.
3 ___ and ___ went to a park.
4 ___ didn't write anything about lunch.
5 ___ was cold.
6 ___ was with someone all day.
7 ___ had a bad day at work.
8 ___ went out at night.
9 ___ went to stores.
10 ___ and ___ didn't eat dinner in a restaurant.

d Look at the highlighted words. With a partner guess their meaning. Check with your teacher or a dictionary.

e Can you find three things in the blogs that you did yesterday?

6 **5.13** **SONG** ♫ *Perfect day*

WORDS AND PHRASES TO LEARN

Did you have a good day?
  It was OK.
the usual
a *wonderful* surprise
spring
paperwork
warm
stressed
a babysitter
Of course.

5C

G simple past: regular verbs
V common verbs 3; more irregular verbs
P regular simple past endings

I arrived in Rome at 11:00.

It changed my life

1 GRAMMAR simple past: regular verbs

a Erasmus is a student exchange program. Every year, thousands of Erasmus students study at a foreign university. Joanna, from Poland, went to Rome last September. Match the sentences and pictures.

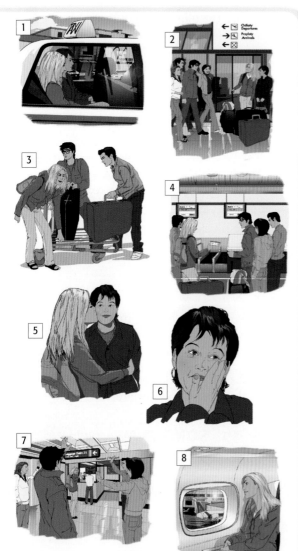

- ☐ I kissed my mother good-bye.
- ☐1☐ I went to the airport with my mother.
- ☐ It was early. We waited at check-in.
- ☐ My friends went to the airport, too.
- ☐ My mother cried.
- ☐ My friends were sad, too. They wanted to come.
- ☐ They helped me with my suitcases.
- ☐ I arrived in Rome at 11:00.

b **5.14** Listen and check. Were you right?

c Write the simple past of these regular verbs.

1 help	_____	4 cry	_____
2 wait	_____	5 want	_____
3 kiss	_____	6 arrive	_____

d ⬭ **p.96 Grammar Bank 5C.** Read the rules and do the exercises.

2 PRONUNCIATION regular simple past endings

a **5.16** Listen and repeat the sounds and sentences.

🐕 d	My mother cried. I arrived in Rome at 11:00.
👕 t	I kissed my mother good-bye. They helped me with my suitcases.
/ɪd/	We waited at check-in. They wanted to come.

b **5.17** Listen and repeat the story in **1a.** Then cover the sentences and look at the pictures. Tell Joanna's story.

3 WRITING & SPEAKING

a What did you do yesterday / last night / this morning? Write true ⊞ or ⊟ sentences.

yesterday	last night	this morning
play a computer game	watch TV	listen to the radio
use the Internet	study English	walk to work / school
check my e-mails	talk to a friend	wait for a bus

b Tell a partner. Did you do the same things?

I didn't play a computer game yesterday. I used the Internet…

4 VOCABULARY common verbs 3

a Can you remember? Match 1–8 to a–h.

1 drive	☐	a	photos
2 see	☐	b	money
3 hear	☐	c	a movie
4 come	☐	d	the piano
5 take	☐	e	by credit card
6 play	☐	f	a noise
7 pay	☐	g	to class
8 change	☐	h	a car

b ⬭ **p.113 Vocabulary Bank** *Common verbs 3.* Do part **A.**

5 READING & SPEAKING

a Look only at the pictures in **1a**. Can you remember Joanna's story?

b Which of these things do you think were problems for Joanna when she arrived in Rome? In pairs, check (✔) your guesses under **My guess**.

	My guess	What Joanna said
where to live	☐	☐
making friends	☐	☐
the weather	☐	☐
the food	☐	☐
the language	☐	☐
Italian men	☐	☐
money	☐	☐
different customs	☐	☐

c Read what Joanna wrote on an Erasmus website. Check (✔) what she said were problems under **What Joanna said**. Were you right?

I lived, I loved, I cried...

I stayed at a hotel the first night. In the morning, I bought a map and went to see the university, and I rented a room in a house. I walked through the city to my classes every morning. Italian men said, "Ciao bella!" I liked it!

I spoke a little Italian from school, but when I arrived in Rome I couldn't understand people. I spoke English or Polish with other Erasmus students. But then I started going to Italian classes, and I also made friends with some Italians. They helped me a lot! After three months, I could speak pretty well. Another problem was that Rome is very expensive, but I found a job in an Irish pub, and I worked three evenings a week.

I learned a lot about Italy and Italians. You can't start the day without "un caffè." Italian food is the best in the world, but don't ask for ketchup! And the number one topic of conversation is politics and soccer.

Erasmus changed my life. I lived a different life in a fantastic city. I met new people from all over the world and made some wonderful friends. I learned to understand another culture. Of course it wasn't all perfect. Living in another country isn't easy, and an Italian man broke my heart!

I came back from Italy a year ago, but a small part of me stayed in Rome. I drink espresso every morning, eat a lot of pasta, and I use my hands a lot when I speak. Now I feel European, not only Polish!

My friends

With Fabio

The Forum

d Read the text again and find the simple past of the verbs. Write **R** (regular) or **I** (irregular).

1	stay	_stayed_	R
2	buy	_____	☐
3	rent	_____	☐
4	say	_____	☐
5	like	_____	☐
6	speak	_____	☐
7	can / can't	_____ / _____	☐
8	start	_____	☐
9	make	_____	☐
10	find	_____	☐
11	learn	_____	☐
12	change	_____	☐
13	live	_____	☐
14	meet	_____	☐
15	break	_____	☐
16	come back	_____	☐

e **5.19** Listen and check. Listen again and repeat.

f Do you know anyone who went to live or study in another country? Where did they go? Did they have a good time?

WORDS AND PHRASES TO LEARN

make friends
break your heart
use your hands
the best in the world
speak Italian pretty well
I feel *European*.
a year / three days / a week ago

5

PRACTICAL ENGLISH

Ordinal numbers
Months
Saying the date

What's the date today?

What's the date today?
It's February seventh.

1 ORDINAL NUMBERS

a Do the quiz with a partner.

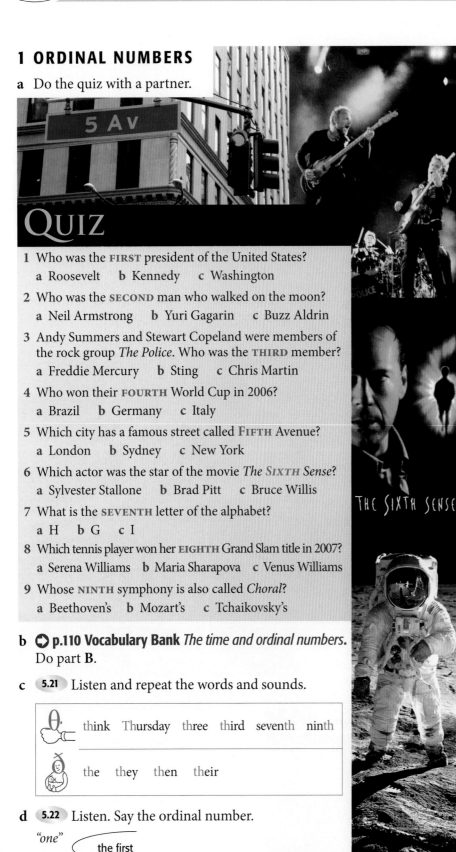

QUIZ

1 Who was the **FIRST** president of the United States?
  a Roosevelt **b** Kennedy **c** Washington

2 Who was the **SECOND** man who walked on the moon?
  a Neil Armstrong **b** Yuri Gagarin **c** Buzz Aldrin

3 Andy Summers and Stewart Copeland were members of the rock group *The Police*. Who was the **THIRD** member?
  a Freddie Mercury **b** Sting **c** Chris Martin

4 Who won their **FOURTH** World Cup in 2006?
  a Brazil **b** Germany **c** Italy

5 Which city has a famous street called **FIFTH** Avenue?
  a London **b** Sydney **c** New York

6 Which actor was the star of the movie *The* **SIXTH** *Sense*?
  a Sylvester Stallone **b** Brad Pitt **c** Bruce Willis

7 What is the **SEVENTH** letter of the alphabet?
  a H **b** G **c** I

8 Which tennis player won her **EIGHTH** Grand Slam title in 2007?
  a Serena Williams **b** Maria Sharapova **c** Venus Williams

9 Whose **NINTH** symphony is also called *Choral*?
  a Beethoven's **b** Mozart's **c** Tchaikovsky's

b ➲ **p.110 Vocabulary Bank** *The time and ordinal numbers.* Do part **B**.

c **5.21** Listen and repeat the words and sounds.

θ	think Thursday three third seventh ninth
ð	the they then their

d **5.22** Listen. Say the ordinal number.

"one" → the first

2 MONTHS

a **5.23** Listen and repeat the months.

JAN	January /ˈdʒænyuɛri/
FEB	February /ˈfɛbyuɛri/
MAR	March /martʃ/
APR	April /ˈeɪprəl/
MAY	May /meɪ/
JUN	June /dʒun/
JUL	July /dʒʊˈlaɪ/
AUG	August /ˈɔɡəst/
SEPT	September /sɛpˈtɛmbər/
OCT	October /akˈtoʊbər/
NOV	November /noʊˈvɛmbər/
DEC	December /dɪˈsɛmbər/

b Cover the months and look at **JAN**, **FEB**, etc. Remember and say the months.

c Cover **a** and answer the questions.

Which month sometimes has 29 days?
Which four months end in *er*?
Which month has only three letters?
Which three months begin with the letter *j*?
Which four months end with the letter *y*?

3 SAYING THE DATE

a `5.24` Listen and complete the dialogues with an ordinal number.

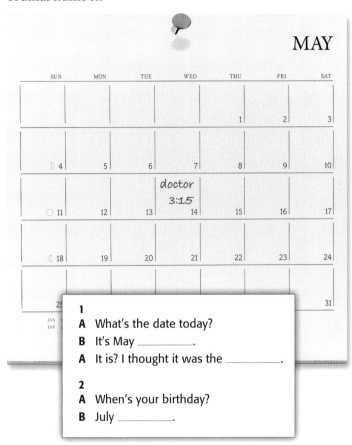

MAY

SUN	MON	TUE	WED	THU	FRI	SAT
				1	2	3
4	5	6	7	8	9	10
11	12	13	14 *doctor 3:15*	15	16	17
18	19	20	21	22	23	24
25						31

1
A What's the date today?
B It's May _____.
A It is? I thought it was the _____.

2
A When's your birthday?
B July _____.

Saying the date

We say	We write
May fourth	May 4th / May 4
July twentieth	7/20

b `5.25` Listen and repeat the dates. Practice saying them.

January 1st	February 3rd	March 5th
April 12th	May 15th	June 22nd
July 31st	August 10th	September 14th
October 9th	November 30th	December 25th

c Ask and answer the questions in pairs.

What's the date today?   What was the date yesterday?

d Stand up. Ask other students *When's your birthday?* Make a class list.

e Tell a partner three birthdays that are important for you.

My mother's birthday is on June 27th.

4 PEOPLE ON THE STREET

> 1 When's your birthday?
> 2 What did you do on your last birthday?

a `5.26` Listen to Corinne. When's her birthday?

b `5.27` Listen. What did she do on her last birthday?

Corinne

Birthday _____
"I had _____."

c `5.28` Listen to four more people. Write their birthdays and complete the sentences.

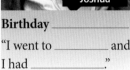
Joshua

Birthday _____
"I went to _____ and I had _____."

Hampton

Birthday _____
"I saw _____."

Christian

Birthday _____
"I can't _____."

Laura

Birthday _____
"I had _____ with some _____."

d In pairs, ask and answer the questions in the box.

WORDS AND PHRASES TO LEARN

What's the date?
It's *May fifth*.
When's your birthday?

GRAMMAR

Circle the correct answer.

Hello, _____ Alex.

a I   (b) I'm

1 It _____ very cold last winter.
   a was   b were

2 Where _____ yesterday at six o'clock?
   a you were   b were you

3 Kelly _____ at work yesterday.
   a wasn't   b weren't

4 I _____ to Brazil last summer.
   a go   b went

5 I got up late, and I _____ breakfast.
   a don't had   b didn't have

6 _____ breakfast this morning?
   a Did you have   b Had you

7 My sister _____ music in college.
   a studyed   b studied

8 They _____ at a cafe.
   a stoped   b stopped

9 What time _____?
   a did they arrive   b did they arrived

10 I _____ a lot of people at the university.
   a meeted   b met

VOCABULARY

a Complete with *in*, *at*, or *on*.

He lives *in* New York.

1 She works _____ home.
2 I was _____ the gym this morning.
3 Are you _____ bed? Get up! It's nine o'clock!
4 I had a sandwich _____ the plane.
5 Marsha wasn't _____ school yesterday. Maybe she's sick.

b Complete with a verb from the list.

arrive	buy	come back	find	~~rent~~	stay

We want to *rent* an apartment downtown.

1 Oh, no! I can't _____ my keys.
2 We _____ in Kyoto on February second.
3 Did you _____ in a hotel in Berlin?
4 When did you _____ from Mexico?
5 I want to _____ a new car. My car is ten years old.

c Write the verbs in the simple past.

live   _____*lived*_____

1 break   _____
2 make   _____
3 play   _____
4 come   _____
5 work   _____

d Write the next word.

one, two, _____*three*_____

1 the first, the second, _____
2 April, May, _____
3 the eighteenth, the nineteenth, _____
4 December, January, _____

e Complete the phrases.

Do you **p**refer tea or coffee?

1 **A** What did you do **l**_____ night?
   B I went to the movies.
2 **A** Did you **h**_____ a good day?
   B It was OK.
3 **A** How was your weekend?
   B Oh, it was the **u**_____.
4 **A** What's the **d**_____ today?
   B It's October first.
5 **A** Do you like Italian food?
   B Yes, it's the **b**_____ food in the world.

PRONUNCIATION

a Can you remember these words and sounds?

vowels

consonants

b ⊙ **p.117 / 119 Sound Bank.** Check the words and sounds, and practice saying the example words.

c Underline the stressed syllable.

Italian

ticket	arrive	seventeenth	September	July

1 CAN YOU UNDERSTAND THIS TEXT?

Desiderius Erasmus was born in Rotterdam in Holland, in 1466 or 1469 – we don't know exactly when. His mother and father died when he was 15 years old. He went to school in Holland, where he was a very good student of Latin. When he finished, he studied at the University of Paris. Later, he worked as a teacher there for some years. After that, he went to England, and he was a professor at Cambridge University. When he was in England, he made many friends, including King Henry VIII. After that, Erasmus traveled all over Europe and lived and worked at universities in many different countries. He studied Greek, and he wrote many books, including famous editions of the Bible in Latin and Greek. Erasmus died in Switzerland on July 12th, 1536. 450 years later, the Erasmus program, where students can study at universities in other countries, was started.

a Read the text about Erasmus and check (✔) the sentences that are true.

1 He was German. ☐
2 His mother and father died when he was a teenager. ☐
3 He went to school in Holland. ☐
4 He studied Latin. ☐
5 He was a teacher in France. ☐
6 He met King Henry VIII. ☐
7 He studied at Cambridge University. ☐
8 He lived in many different countries. ☐
9 He was a writer. ☐
10 He died when he was 50. ☐

b Look at the highlighted words and phrases and guess their meaning. Check with your teacher or a dictionary.

2 CAN YOU WRITE THIS IN ENGLISH?

a Read the blog. Did Kim have a good day?

Posted: Monday

What did people all over the world do last Sunday?
Write your blog for our history website.

Last Sunday, I got up at 9:30 in the morning. I had a cup of coffee and read the Sunday newspaper. Then I made breakfast. We had eggs and sausage. We always have a big breakfast on Sunday, but we don't have lunch.

In the afternoon, the weather was beautiful, and we went for a long walk in the park.

In the evening, when our son was in bed, my husband and I made dinner together. Then we talked about our day and laughed a lot. We went to bed early because we were tired, and we start work early on Monday.

Comments 8

b Write a blog for a history website. Say what you did last Sunday.

3 CAN YOU UNDERSTAND THESE PEOPLE?

5.29 Listen and choose the right answer.

1 Where was Andy last night?
   a At his friend's house.   b At the movies.
2 What did Rebecca like about the hotel?
   a The rooms.   b The breakfast.
3 Where did Owen work yesterday?
   a In his office.   b At home.
4 What did Emma see last night?
   a An Italian movie.   b A French movie.
5 Where did Jane stay in Acapulco?
   a At a hotel.   b In a rented apartment.
6 _____ bought something at the new shopping mall.
   a One of the women   b The two women
7 What did Alan do on Saturday?
   a He did housework.   b He made lunch.
8 When is Liam's birthday?
   a June 10th.   b June 11th.

4 CAN YOU SAY THIS IN ENGLISH?

Check (✔) the boxes.

Can you…?

say where you were yesterday ☐ Yes, I can.
say what you did yesterday ☐ Yes, I can.
ask what other people did yesterday ☐ Yes, I can.
say dates ☐ Yes, I can.

6 A

G there is / there are
V hotels; in, on, under
P /ɛr/ and /ɪr/

There isn't a TV, but there are some books.

On an island in Alaska

1 VOCABULARY hotels

a Look at these things from a hotel room. What are they?

1 It's a chair.

b ➲ **p.114 Vocabulary Bank** *Hotels.*

1   2   3   4   5   6   7

2 GRAMMAR there is / there are

a **6.3** Listen to two people who arrive at a hotel on an island in Alaska. Are they happy with the hotel and with their room? Why (not)?

b Listen again and read the dialogue. Complete the missing words.

c Read the dialogue again. Underline examples of *there is / are* ⊞, ⊟, and ⍰.

d ➲ **p.98 Grammar Bank 6A.** Read the rules and do the exercises.

e Practice the dialogue in **2b** in groups of three.

f **6.5** Listen to what happens next. Do they leave? Why (not)? Do you like this hotel? Why (not)?

3 PRONUNCIATION /ɛr/ and /ɪr/

a **6.6** Listen and repeat the words and sounds.

ɛr	where	there	airport	upstairs
ɪr	near	here	year	we're

b Make true ⊞ or ⊟ sentences.

in your classroom
a board   windows   a table   a TV
chairs   a lamp   pictures   computers

in your school
a library   a cafe   bathrooms   a parking lot

There's a board.

There aren't any windows.

Man	Hello. We have a reservation.
Receptionist	Let's see, yes, Mr. and Mrs. Robson. Welcome to the island. Your ¹ *room*'s upstairs, number seven.
Woman	Is there an ² _____?
Receptionist	No, I'm sorry, there isn't. But I can help you with your suitcases.
Receptionist	This is your room.
Woman	It's very small.
Receptionist	Yes, but there's a ³ _____ view.
Man	There are ⁴ _____ _____. We wanted a double bed.
Receptionist	I'm sorry, there aren't any rooms with a double bed.
Woman	Where's the TV?
Receptionist	There isn't one. There are some ⁵ _____ over there.
Woman	Books!
Receptionist	This is the bathroom.
Woman	There isn't a ⁶ _____.
Receptionist	No, there's a ⁷ _____. It uses less water.
Man	Can I use the Internet here?
Receptionist	No, I'm sorry you can't.
Woman	Are there any ⁸ _____ near here?
Receptionist	No, ma'am, there aren't. Enjoy your stay.

4 READING

a Look at photos of three unusual hotels. Match the photos and information.

b Read the information about the three hotels. Check (✔) the boxes.

	A	B	C
1 You can go with children.	✔	✔	✔
2 There's a swimming pool.	☐	☐	☐
3 There is only one restaurant.	☐	☐	☐
4 You can't stay only one night.	☐	☐	☐
5 You arrive by boat or plane.	☐	☐	☐
6 You can see fish from your room.	☐	☐	☐
7 You can have a massage there.	☐	☐	☐
8 You can have a meal in your room when you want.	☐	☐	☐

c Do you like the hotels? Which one do you prefer?

Hotels with a difference

A UNDER the water: Poseidon Resort, Fiji

A resort island in the Pacific Ocean. You arrive by private boat or plane. Stay in a room on the island, or take an elevator down and stay in a room 40 feet underwater. You can watch and feed fish from your room! There are activities on the island for children and adults.

Location: Poseidon Mystery Island, Fiji
Number of rooms: 73
Price: $15,000 – $30,000 per week
• 6 restaurants
• swimming pool
• spa and gym

B IN a mountain: Elkep Evi, Turkey

Ancient caves in the side of a mountain, now hotel rooms with modern facilities. Most rooms have a private terrace with fantastic views of Cappadocia. Turkish breakfast served in the garden.

Location: Ürgüp, Cappadocia, Central Turkey
Number of rooms: 21
Price: Under $225
• spa with massages and treatments
• 24-hour room service
• restaurant
• children welcome

C ON an island: Kamalame Cay, Bahamas

Luxury private island with three miles of beautiful beach. You can only get to the island by our private boat or seaplane. Fantastic Caribbean cuisine, a perfect relaxing vacation.

Location: Kamalame Cay, Andros, Bahamas
Number of rooms: 16
Price: $840 – $3,900
• gourmet restaurant
• 24-hour room service
• swimming pool
• family bedrooms
• children welcome

5 SPEAKING

a Write *in*, *on*, or *under* for pictures 1–3.

  1   2   3

c ◗ **Communication** *Is there a TV? Where is it? A p.77 B p.80.* Draw things in the hotel rooms.

b Ask and answer in pairs about the remote control.

1   2   3   4   5   6

Where's the remote control?

It's on the TV.

WORDS AND PHRASES TO LEARN

Welcome to *the island*.
on the first floor
up<u>stairs</u> / down<u>stairs</u>
En<u>joy</u> your stay.
in *the cabinet*
on *the bed*
<u>un</u>der *the chair*
There's a beautiful view.
a boat

6

B

G *there was / there were*
V places
P the letters *ea*

> There was a beautiful beach.
> There weren't any hotels.

Dream town?

1 VOCABULARY places

a Can you remember? Do the quiz with a partner.

Places quiz
Where do you go…?

1 when you want to have lunch or dinner
2 when you have an accident
3 when you want to park your car
4 when you want to buy something
5 when you want to learn something
6 when you want to stay the night in another town

b ➡ **p.115 Vocabulary Bank** *Places*.

2 READING & LISTENING

a Read about Benidorm and answer the questions.

1 Was Benidorm big or small in the 1950s?
2 Who was Pedro Zaragoza?
3 What did he want Benidorm to be?
4 What did he build?
5 What rule did he change?

b **6.8** Listen to a journalist talking to a local historian. Complete the information about Benidorm.

Benidorm today	Benidorm in the 1950s
There are 65,000 _people_ living in Benidorm.	There were only 3,000.
There are four million _____ a year.	There were 300.
There's an _____ 35 miles from Benidorm.	There wasn't one.
There are 128 _____.	There were three.
There are 264 _____.	There weren't any.

c Do you prefer Benidorm today or in the 1950s? Why? Are there any places in your country like Benidorm?

Benidorm in the 1950s

One man's dream

In the 1950s, Benidorm in southeast Spain was a small fishing village. But the mayor of Benidorm, Pedro Zaragoza, had a dream. He wanted Benidorm to be a big tourist town. He started to build hotels. In the 1950s, women couldn't wear a bikini on the beach in Spain. Mayor Zaragoza changed the bikini rule in Benidorm. In 1959, the first tourists from Northern Europe started to arrive…

Benidorm today

3 GRAMMAR

there was / there were

a Look at the sentences in **Benidorm today** and **Benidorm in the 1950s** on page 56. What is the past of *there is* and *there are*, and *there isn't* and *there aren't*?

b ⊙ **p.98 Grammar Bank 6B.** Read the rules and do the exercises.

4 PRONUNCIATION

the letters *ea*

a `6.10` Put the words in the right column. Listen and check.

beach	bread	please	breakfast
eat	east	speak	

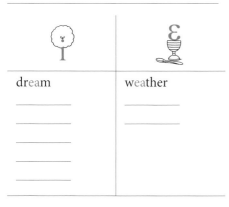

dream	weather
_____	_____
_____	_____
_____	_____
_____	_____

b `6.11` Listen. Practice the sentences.

My dream is to speak perfect English.
Please eat your breakfast.
The weather at the beach was terrible.

WELCOME TO
Benidorm

5 LISTENING

a `6.12` Jeff and Kelly are from the United States. They are on vacation in the UK. Listen to Kelly talking to an English friend. Did they have a good weekend?

b Listen again. Circle the right answer, a or b.

1 a They went to Benidorm. b They went to Blackpool.
2 a They went in April. b They went in May.
3 a Some restaurants weren't open. b Some restaurants were very expensive.
4 a Jeff wanted to stay in a hotel. b Jeff wanted to stay in a bed and breakfast.
5 a They wanted cereal. b They wanted eggs, sausage, and toast.
6 a There wasn't any coffee. b There wasn't any tea.

6 SPEAKING & WRITING

a ⊙ **Communication** *Good or bad vacation? A p.78 B p.80.* Role-play a conversation about a vacation.

b Imagine you stayed in a hotel last weekend. It was a disaster. Write an e-mail to a friend. Use the information in the feedback form.

Beach Hotel FEEDBACK FORM

☹

room	hotel
small and cold	receptionist not very friendly
no TV	no restaurant
no towels in the bathroom	a gym but closed

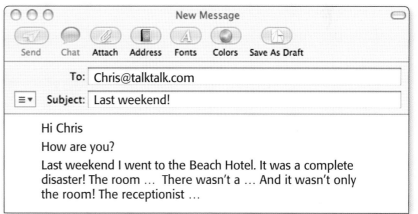

New Message

Send Chat Attach Address Fonts Colors Save As Draft

To: Chris@talktalk.com

Subject: Last weekend!

Hi Chris

How are you?

Last weekend I went to the Beach Hotel. It was a complete disaster! The room … There wasn't a … And it wasn't only the room! The receptionist …

WORDS AND PHRASES TO LEARN
have an <u>a</u>ccident   miles
build (simple past *built*)
wear (simple past *wore*)
How was your *weekend*?
A com<u>ple</u>te di<u>sas</u>ter!
<u>typ</u>ically *English*
a bed and breakfast

6C
G review of simple past; object pronouns: *me*, *him*, etc.
V common verbs 3
P sentence stress

> I saw her on the platform.
> She sat down next to me.

Strangers on a train

1 VOCABULARY common verbs 3

a Can you remember? Complete the questions with a verb from the list.

arrive buy learn meet rent say stay

1 Do you want to _____ another language? Which language?
2 When do you usually _____ your friends? What do you do?
3 What time do you usually _____ at work / school?
4 How do you _____ *Nice to meet you* in your language?
5 Do you _____ your house / apartment?
6 Did you _____ in a hotel on your last vacation? Was it good?
7 Do you _____ things on the Internet? What?

b Answer the questions with a partner.

c ⊙ **p.113 Vocabulary Bank** *Common verbs 3*. Do part **B**.

d Complete with the opposite verbs.

1 The plane **arrives** at 6:00.
   The plane _____ at 6:00.
2 Did you **lose** your bag?
   Did you _____ your bag?
3 I **send** a lot of e-mails.
   I _____ a lot of e-mails.
4 I **get** a lot of birthday presents.
   I _____ a lot of birthday presents.
5 Please **turn on** the TV.
   Please _____ the TV.

2 READING & LISTENING

a **6.14** Read and listen to the story. Answer the questions after each part.

STRANGERS ON A TRAIN

Part 1

When the train stopped, I opened my eyes and looked out of the window. I saw her on the platform. A tall, blond woman with dark blue eyes. The train left the station. As usual, the 6:20 was full.

"Excuse me. Can I sit here?" I opened my eyes again. It was the tall, blond woman.

"Sure," I said. She sat down next to me. There was a nice smell. Chanel Number 5, I thought.

I opened my book and started to read.

"I loved that book."

"Excuse me?" I said.

"I said I loved that book."

We chatted about books until the train arrived at South Station.

"Coffee?" she said.

I looked at my watch. "OK," I said.

1 Where did the man first see the woman?
2 What was the woman's perfume?
3 What did they talk about?
4 What did they do when the train arrived?

Part 2

We sat at the station cafe, and we drank coffee and talked. Her name was Olivia. She told me that she worked in Boston.

"What do you do?" I asked.

"I work in real estate – apartments and houses. What do you do?"

"'I work for Citibank."

"That's interesting!" said Olivia. "Do you live in Boston?"

"Yes. I have an apartment near the river." I told her the street.

"Wow! That's an expensive part of Boston!"

I looked at my watch. "It's late. Time to go."

"I can drive you home," she said. "I live near you." She smiled. Her eyes were very blue.

5 What does Olivia do?
6 What does the man do?
7 Where does he live?
8 Where does Olivia live?

b **6.15** Why didn't Olivia come to the theater? What do you think? Now listen to the end of the story. What happened?

c **6.16** Find the simple past of these irregular verbs. Then listen and repeat.

Part 1 see _____   leave _____   think _____
Part 2 drink _____   tell _____
Part 3 drive _____   give _____
Part 4 read _____ /rɛd/   send _____

d ◉ **p.116 Vocabulary Bank** *Irregular verbs.*

STRANGERS ON A TRAIN

Part 3

Her car was in the parking lot. It was an Audi TT.
"Nice car," I said.
She drove fast. Very fast.
She stopped outside my apartment. We said good-bye, and I gave her my phone number.
The next morning there was a text message from Olivia.

I really want to c u again! Friday?

On Friday morning, she called me.
"I have two tickets for *Chicago* tonight at the Colonial Theater! Can you get them from the box office at 7:15? We can meet in the theater cafe at 7:30. The show starts at 8:00."

9 What kind of car does Olivia have?
10 What did she write in the text message?
11 What show did she have tickets for?
12 Where did she want to meet him? What time?

Part 4

I arrived at the theater at 7:00. I got the tickets, and I waited in the cafe. I read a newspaper. Olivia didn't come. I looked at my watch. It was 7:45. I looked at my phone. There was a text message.

Sorry! In a meeting. See you in the theater. Leave my ticket at the box office.

I left her ticket at the box office and found my seat. The show started, but Olivia didn't arrive.
At intermission, I called her, but her phone was off.
I sent her another text:

Where r u?

I was angry. I left the theater and went home. I opened the door of my apartment and turned on the light…

13 What time did he arrive at the theater?
14 What happened at 7:45? What did the man do?
15 What did the man do at intermission?
16 What did he do after that?

---

3 GRAMMAR   object pronouns: *me, him,* etc.

a Look at these sentences from the story. Complete them with a pronoun from the list.

her   me   them   you

1 She sat down next to _____.
2 "I can drive _____ home," she said.
3 I have two tickets for *Chicago*. Can you get _____ from the box office at 7:15?
4 I called _____, but her phone was off.

b Complete the chart with the pronouns in **a**.

Subject pronoun	Object pronoun
I	_____
you	_____
he	him
she	_____
it	it
we	us
they	_____

c ◉ **p.98 Grammar Bank 6C.** Read the rules and do the exercises.

4 PRONUNCIATION   sentence stress

a Match questions 1–5 with answers a–e.

1 Did you see the movie? ☐
2 Did you buy the books? ☐
3 Did you meet Ana? ☐
4 Did John call you? ☐
5 Did Silvia tell you about the party? ☐

a <u>Yes</u>, I <u>bought</u> them <u>yesterday</u>.
b <u>Yes</u>, I <u>met</u> her <u>yesterday</u>.
c <u>Yes</u>, she <u>told</u> us <u>yesterday</u>.
d <u>Yes</u>, he <u>called</u> me <u>yesterday</u>.
e <u>Yes</u>, I <u>saw</u> it <u>yesterday</u>.

b **6.19** Listen and check. Then listen and repeat a–e. <u>C</u>opy the <u>rh</u>ythm.

c Practice with a partner. **A** ask 1–5 in a different order. **B** answer from memory. Then change roles.

5 **6.20** SONG ♫ *I'm a believer*

WORDS AND PHRASES TO LEARN	
full (opposite = <u>empty</u>)	That's <u>interesting</u>.
next to *me*	a text (<u>message</u>)
<u>platform</u>	a show
seat	<u>angry</u>
Time to go.	

What do you think of it?

What do you think of it?
I like it. It's great.

1 ASKING FOR & GIVING OPINIONS

a **6.21** Cover the dialogue and listen. Who likes the music?

A Listen to this. What do you think of it?
B I don't like it. It's awful. Who is it?
A Shakira. I really like her. She's great.

b **6.22** Listen and repeat the dialogue. Which two words have "extra" stress?

c **6.23** Listen and repeat the expressions in the chart for giving opinions about music (column 1).

d **6.24** Listen to eight music extracts. What do you think of them?

Giving opinions: What do you think of…?

	1	2	3	4
☺☺☺	I really like it. It's fantastic / It's great.	I really like _her_. ___ fantastic / ___ great.	I really like ___. ___ fantastic / ___ great.	I really like ___. ___ fantastic / ___ great.
☺☺	I like it.	I like ___.	I like ___.	I like ___.
☹	It's OK.	___ OK.	___ OK.	___ OK.
☹	I don't like it.	I don't like ___.	I don't like ___.	I don't like ___.
☹☹	It's terrible / It's awful.	___ terrible / ___ awful.	___ terrible / ___ awful.	___ terrible / ___ awful.

e Complete the expressions for columns 2–4.

f In pairs, ask and answer about the singers and groups in the photos.

What do you think of Rihanna?

I really like her. She's great.

What do you think of Coldplay?

I don't know them.

Justin Timberlake
Enrique Iglesias
The Rolling Stones
Bob Dylan
Shakira
Nelly Furtado
Coldplay
Avril Lavigne
Beyoncé
Rihanna

g Write names in the spaces. Try to think of songs / people who are very famous.

female singers
_____
_____

male singers
_____
_____

groups
_____
_____

songs
_____
_____

h Ask your partner's opinion of the singers and groups.

2 PEOPLE ON THE STREET

1 What's the last movie you saw?
2 What did you think of it?

a **6.25** Listen to Lauren. What was the last movie she saw?

b **6.26** Listen. What did she think of it?

c **6.27** Listen and answer the questions for the other five people.

A *Lars and the Real Girl* D *Mamma Mia!*
B *WALL·E* E *Wanted*
C *The Visitor* F *Indiana Jones*

Lauren
1 ☐
2 "I thought it was _____."

Dax
1 ☐
2 "I _____ a lot. It was _____ interesting."

Paul
1 ☐
2 "It was _____."

Corinne
1 ☐
2 "I _____ it. I thought it was very _____."

Anna
1 ☐
2 "It was _____."

Joshua
1 ☐
2 "I thought it was _____."

d In pairs, ask and answer the questions in the box.

WORDS AND PHRASES TO LEARN
What do you think of …?
I really like it.
It's fantastic / great.
It's OK.
I don't like it.
It's terrible / <u>aw</u>ful.
What's the last movie you saw?

GRAMMAR

Circle the correct answer.

Hello, _____ Alex.
a I   (b) I'm

1 _____ two beds in the room.
   a There is   b There are
2 There aren't _____ elevators.
   a some   b any
3 Is there _____ lamp on the table?
   a a   b any
4 _____ a lot of tourists in the 1950s.
   a There wasn't   b There weren't
5 _____ a gym in the hotel?
   a There was   b Was there
6 There were _____ people on the beach.
   a some   b any
7 I wrote to John, but _____ didn't answer.
   a he   b him
8 She was in my class, but I don't remember _____.
   a she   b her
9 **A** What do you think of the Beatles?
   B I don't like _____.
   a him   b them
10 I really like Mike, but I don't think he likes _____.
   a my   b me

VOCABULARY

a Write the missing hotel words.

I want to exercise. Is there a **gym** in this hotel?

1 I can't turn on the TV. I can't find the **r**_____ **c**_____.
2 There isn't a **p**_____ on my bed.
3 We want a room with a **d**_____ bed.
4 Excuse me. There aren't any **t**_____, and I want to take a shower.
5 You can leave your car in the **p**_____ **l**_____.

b Write the places.

a place where people can look at
old or interesting things   *museum*

1 a place where you can get gas   _____
2 a small place with only 1,000 people living there   _____
3 the place where you go when you want to travel by plane   _____
4 a place where you can send letters   _____
5 a place where you can buy different kinds of food   _____

c Complete with a common verb from the list.

call   get   give   leave   send   turn off

Did you *get* an e-mail from the hotel?

1 What did your sister _____ you for your birthday?
2 What time did you _____ home this morning?
3 Can you _____ me at home tonight?
4 Remember to _____ your cell phone before you go into class.
5 Did you _____ her an e-mail about the party?

d Write the irregular verbs in the simple past.

know   *knew*

1 drink   _____
2 take   _____
3 tell   _____
4 say   _____
5 leave   _____

e Complete the phrases.

Do you **p***refer* tea or coffee?

1 Your room's on the first **f**_____.
2 My room has a beautiful **v**_____ of the mountains.
3 We can't **w**_____ jeans at my school.
4 It's **t**_____ to go. Bye.
5 What did you think **o**_____ the movie?

PRONUNCIATION

a Can you remember these words and sounds?

vowels

consonants

b ➡ **p.117 / 119 Sound Bank.** Check the words and sounds, and practice saying the example words.

c Underline the stressed syllable.
Italian

bedroom   restaurant   museum   airport   fantastic

1 CAN YOU UNDERSTAND THIS TEXT?

Our week in a treehouse

In April last year, we stayed for a week at the Safariland Treehouse Resort in southern India. It was a wonderful experience!

Our room was up in a tree. We climbed stairs to get to it! The room was very nice. We had a large bed and pillows. There was a bathroom in the room. There wasn't a bathtub, but there was a shower. We even had hot water! It was hot at night, but we slept well.

We had breakfast, lunch, and dinner at the resort. But there was a problem. You couldn't bring any food to the resort. The meals were at the same time every day. I was hungry late at night, but there wasn't any food!

What is there to do at the resort? There aren't any TVs or computers, but there is a lot to do outside. You can walk in the forest or climb a mountain. You can play sports at the resort, too. They have soccer, tennis, and volleyball games. There's a park for children at the resort. My daughter loved it!

We had a great time at the resort, but one week was enough!

Neil Friedman

a Read about a tourist's experience at a resort. Mark the sentences T (true) or F (false).

1 There was a shower and a bathtub in the bathroom.
2 It wasn't cold at night.
3 It was difficult to sleep at night.
4 Neil didn't bring food to the resort.
5 You can't watch TV at the resort.
6 Neil's daughter liked the park.
7 Neil wanted to stay another week.

b Look at the highlighted words and phrases and guess their meaning. Check with your teacher or a dictionary.

2 CAN YOU WRITE THIS IN ENGLISH?

a Read about Masami's vacation. Answer the questions.

Paragraph 1
1 Where did she go?
2 When did she go?
3 How did she travel?

Paragraph 2
4 Where did she stay?
5 What did she do?
6 What did she see?

Paragraph 3
7 Does she recommend it? Why?

A Great Vacation

I went to Mexico last year with my husband. We went by plane.

First we stayed in Cancún. Our hotel was really nice, and there was a big swimming pool. There was a beautiful beach, too. We swam every day, and the ocean was very warm. Then we traveled around the Yucatán Peninsula by bus. We saw Chichen Itza. It was fantastic.

I recommend Mexico. It's a beautiful country, the people are very friendly, and the weather is great.

Masami Tanaka in Osaka

b Write three paragraphs about a vacation. Answer the questions in **a** for you.

3 CAN YOU UNDERSTAND THESE PEOPLE?

6.28 Listen to a woman calling Vacation Homes Limited and choose the right answer.

1 The village is _____ miles from Bordeaux.
   a 13   b 30
2 The village is _____.
   a near the beach   b in the mountains
3 There are _____ bedrooms.
   a three   b four
4 One of the bedrooms is _____.
   a very small   b very big
5 a There's one bathroom.
   b There are two bathrooms.
6 The woman wants to go on vacation from September _____.
   a 10th–20th   b 12th–22nd
7 She can meet the man from Vacation Homes on _____.
   a Tuesday   b Thursday
8 Vacation Homes is at number _____ Cowley Road.
   a 86   b 68

> **VACATION HOMES LIMITED**
>
> Large house to rent with pool in beautiful French village. For more information call 645-3721.
> **reference 4795**

4 CAN YOU SAY THIS IN ENGLISH?

Check (✔) the boxes.
Can you…?

identify things in a hotel room	☐ Yes, I can.
ask about facilities in a hotel	☐ Yes, I can.
say what there is in your town	☐ Yes, I can.
describe how your town was in the past	☐ Yes, I can.
give your opinion about people and things	☐ Yes, I can.

7 A
G present continuous
V verbs and verb phrases
P /ʊ/, /u/, and /ŋ/

> What's she doing?
> She's playing the piano.

What are they doing?

1 GRAMMAR present continuous

a **7.1** Listen to two people on a TV game show. Fill in the blanks.

Host	OK, David and Kim. You have [1]*one* minute. What are they doing?
David	Is it a man or a woman?
Kim	It's a woman. Look at her hair. What's she doing?
David	Is she playing the [2]_____?
Kim	No, she isn't. She's using a [3]_____.
David	Yes, OK. I think you're right. And the next one?
Kim	It's a man and a woman. They're eating [4]_____.
David	No, they aren't eating [5]_____. They're eating [6]_____ food.
Host	Time's up, Kim and David. Are those your answers?
David	Yes, they are.
Host	OK. So what do you think? Are they right or wrong?

b Look at the pictures. What do <u>you</u> think? What is she doing in the picture on the left? What are they doing in the picture on the right?

c **7.2** Listen and check. Are Kim and David right or wrong?

d ◯ **p.100 Grammar Bank 7A.** Read the rules and do the exercises.

2 PRONUNCIATION /ʊ/, /u/, and /ŋ/

a **7.4** Listen and repeat the words and sounds.

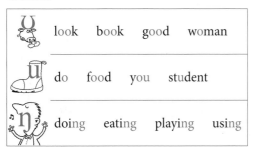

look	book	good	woman
do	food	you	student
doing	eating	playing	using

b Read the dialogue in **1a**. Practice it in groups of three.

c Look at pictures 1–6. Practice with a partner.

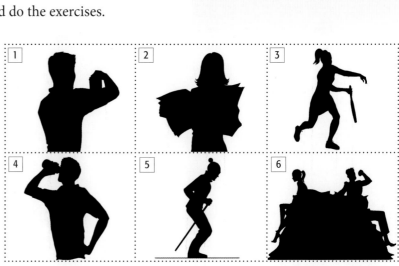

> What's he doing?

> He's …

3 VOCABULARY verbs and verb phrases

a **7.5** Listen and repeat the verbs and verb phrases in 1–8.

b Complete the phrases with a verb from **a**.

1 _travel_ by train
2 _____ a marathon
3 _____ in tents
4 _____ a bike
5 _____ the tango
6 _____ a suitcase
7 _____ on the sofa
8 _____ all weekend

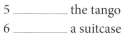

1 run   2 carry *a bag*   3 lie *on the floor*

4 dance   5 ride *a horse*   6 camp   7 rain   8 travel

4 READING

a Joe is traveling in Asia with friends. Look at his photos. Then read the sentences and write the letter of the photo.

1 There are flowers on the table. ☐
2 It's raining. ☐
3 One of the people is carrying a red bag. ☐
4 They're looking at the camera. ☐ ☐
5 A woman is carrying a bottle of water. ☐
6 You can see the ocean. ☐ ☐
7 They are wearing coats. ☐

b Cover the sentences. Look at the photos and say the sentences.

c Now read Joe's blog. Mark the sentences T (true) or F (false).

1 They only spent a weekend in Ho Chi Minh City.
2 They traveled to Mui Ne by bus.
3 They are staying in an expensive hotel.
4 Yesterday they had lunch and dinner at a restaurant.
5 They rode bikes along the Great Ocean Road.
6 They only stayed in Mui Ne for three days.
7 They are now in Saigon.

d Look at the highlighted words and guess their meaning. Check with your teacher or a dictionary.

5 SPEAKING

a Write the names of six people (family or friends). What do you think they are doing right now?

b Tell your partner about your people. Are any of them doing the same thing?

My sister is taking her daughter to school.

I think my mother is…

We're in Vietnam, and we're having a great time. After five days in Ho Chi Minh City, we needed a relaxing break. We arrived in Mui Ne after six hours on the bus. We found a three star hotel on the beach with a swimming pool. It is very cheap – only $30 dollars a night, including breakfast! We can see and hear the ocean from our room.

Mui Ne is beautiful! The beach is clean, and the water is really warm. We lie on the beach all day, drink fresh fruit juice, and swim. Yesterday we had lunch in a small restaurant on the beach. The fish and seafood were wonderful. We met some really nice people from Australia. They are traveling around the world. After lunch, we all rented motorcycles and drove along the Great Ocean Road. We had dinner together, a barbecue on the beach, and two of the boys played their guitars. We danced and sang.

We planned to stay in Mui Ne for only three days, but we are still here. We don't want to leave! We're planning to stay two more days, and then go to Saigon. Watch this space!

WORDS AND PHRASES TO LEARN

including	seafood
clean	barbecue
fresh	still

7 B

G future: *be going to* (plans)
V future time expressions
P sentence stress

Trip of a lifetime

What are you going to do?
I'm going to ride a bike from Ecuador to Argentina.

1 GRAMMAR future: *be going to* (plans)

a **7.6** Liz has plans for a very special trip. Read and listen to the dialogue. Complete it with the verbs in the list.

be camp come back ~~ride~~ go (x2) start stay

Jerry What exactly are your plans, Liz?
Liz I'm going to ¹ *ride* a bike from Ecuador to Argentina.
Jerry Wow! How far is that?
Liz It's about 4,700 miles.
Jerry Are you going to ² _____ alone?
Liz No, I'm not. I'm going to ³ _____ with a friend.
Jerry Where are you going to ⁴ _____?
Liz We're going to ⁵ _____, and maybe sometimes stay in small hotels.
Jerry When are you going to ⁶ _____ your trip?
Liz In October. And we aren't going to ⁷ _____ until April.
Jerry Six months – that's a long time! Are you excited?
Liz Yes, I am. It's going to ⁸ _____ a great trip!

b Read the dialogue again. Are the highlighted sentences about the present, the past, or the future?

c Complete the sentences in the chart.

⊞ I'm _____ _____ ride a bike from Ecuador to Argentina.	
⸮ _____ _____ going to go alone?	
⊟ We _____ _____ _____ come back until April.	

d ⊙ **p.100 Grammar Bank 7B.** Read the rules and do the exercises.

2 PRONUNCIATION sentence stress

a **7.8** Listen to these sentences from the dialogue. <u>Underline</u> the stressed words.

I'm going to ride a bike from Ecuador to Argentina.
Are you going to go alone?
Where are you going to stay?

b **7.9** Listen and repeat the highlighted sentences in the dialogue. Copy the rhythm.

c In pairs, practice the dialogue.

d **7.10** Listen and make ⊞ sentences with *going to* about tomorrow.

"go to work"
I'm going to go to work tomorrow.

e What are <u>you</u> going to do tomorrow? Write five things you are going to do, four true and one false. Read them to a partner. Can he / she guess which thing is false?

Tomorrow I'm going to get up at 6:30.
I'm going to have lunch with my friend Ana…

3 VOCABULARY & SPEAKING

a Write the time expressions in the right place on the time line.

| tomorrow | next year | next week | tomorrow night | ~~tonight~~ | next month |

tonight

now → the future

b Look at the questionnaire below. What words are missing? Think about your answers to the questions.

QUESTIONNAIRE

Today
Where / go after class?
/ go out this evening?
What time / go to bed tonight?

Tomorrow
/ get up early tomorrow?
What / do tomorrow morning?
Where / have lunch?

On the weekend
/ go somewhere? Where?
/ go shopping?
/ go out on Saturday evening?
What / do?

In the summer / next year
/ go on vacation?
Where / go?
Who / go with?

c Work in pairs. **A** ask **B** about his / her plans for **today**, **tomorrow**, etc.

4 LISTENING

a Cover the dialogue in exercise **1**. In pairs, remember Liz's plans for her trip.

Ecuador–Argentina; friend;
camp; October; April

> She's going to ride a bike from Ecuador to Argentina.

b **7.11** Liz came back from her trip to South America last week. Listen and number the photos in the order she mentions them.

c Listen again and mark the sentences T (true) or F (false). Then correct the wrong information.

1 Liz and her friend finished their trip.
2 They rode bikes all the way.
3 They always camped in Ecuador and Peru.
4 Liz's bike broke when they were near La Paz.
5 Liz's friend repaired the bike.
6 Their favorite place was Patagonia.
7 For their next trip, they're going to go to Australia.

Camping with an alpaca!

Argentina!

Bike problems

The bus in Chile

5 SPEAKING

a Plan your dream trip. Think of answers to the questions below.

Where / go? _____
When / go? _____
How / travel? _____ (by bus, by plane, etc.)
Who / with? _____
Where / stay? _____

WORDS AND PHRASES TO LEARN

How far is that?
un*til April*
tomorrow night
next month
next year
That's a long time.

b Ask a partner about his / her trip. Which trip do you prefer?

> Where are you going to go?

> I'm going to go to Egypt.

G future: *be going to* (predictions)
V the weather; review: verb collocation
P review of sounds

It's going to rain.
It isn't going to snow.

What's going to happen?

1 GRAMMAR   future: *be going to* (predictions)

a Match the sentences and pictures.

- [ ] It's going to be hot.
- [ ] It's going to be sunny.
- [ ] It's going to be cold.
- [ ] It's going to snow.
- [ ] It's going to rain.

b **7.12** Listen to a weather forecast for tomorrow. Draw the symbols on the map.

c Write two sentences about tomorrow's weather where you are.

d ➲ **p.100 Grammar Bank 7C.** Read the rules and do the exercises.

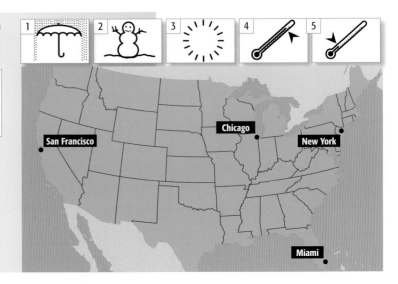

2 SPEAKING

a Look at the picture of the park. What do you think is going to happen? Write sentences for 1–8. You are going to find out later if you are right.

b Compare your predictions with another pair. Are they the same?

3 PRONUNCIATION   review of sounds

a Can you remember? Put three verbs in each column.

camp   do   get   go   have   know   lose   make   meet   play   rain   relax   rent   see   send   snow   speak   use

b **7.14** Listen and check.

4 VOCABULARY & SPEAKING   review: verb collocation

a Can you remember? Which verbs do you use?

do   get   go   have   make   meet   play   take

1 _____ an umbrella a photo a shower	2 _____ up in the morning an e-mail	3 _____ home shopping on vacation	4 _____ dinner a sandwich children

5 _____ homework housework	6 _____ the guitar basketball computer games	7 _____ friends a mistake dinner	8 _____ somebody for the first time some friends after class

b Complete the questions with a verb from **a**.

1 Do you _____ sports? What sports do you _____?
2 What do you usually _____ for breakfast? What did you _____ for breakfast this morning?
3 When do you usually _____ housework? Are you going to _____ housework tonight?
4 Do you sometimes _____ dinner for your friends or family? What do you usually _____?
5 Did you _____ on vacation last summer? Where did you _____?
6 Do you _____ a lot of e-mails? How many do you _____ a day?
7 Where did you _____ your best friend? When did you _____?
8 When do you _____ photos? Do you usually _____ photos with a camera or with your cell phone?

c Ask and answer the questions with a partner.

5 **7.15** SONG ♫ *Three little birds*

7

PRACTICAL ENGLISH

Asking for and giving directions
Prepositions of place
Polite intonation

Is there a bank near here?

> Is there a bank near here?
> Yes, go straight ahead, and turn left. It's on the right.

1 ASKING WHERE PLACES ARE

a **7.16** Listen and repeat the words.

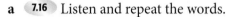

1		2		3		4	
next to		across from		between		on the corner	

b **7.17** Look at the map. Listen and name the places.

school	post office	supermarket		bank	music store	theater
park	museum	church		bookstore	pharmacy	movie theater

c Practice in pairs.

> Where's the park?

> It's across from the school.

d **7.18** Look at the map and the names of the streets and buildings. Listen and complete the dialogue with two places.

A Excuse me. Is there a ¹_____ near here?
B Yes, there's one on South Street, next to the ²_____.
A Thanks.

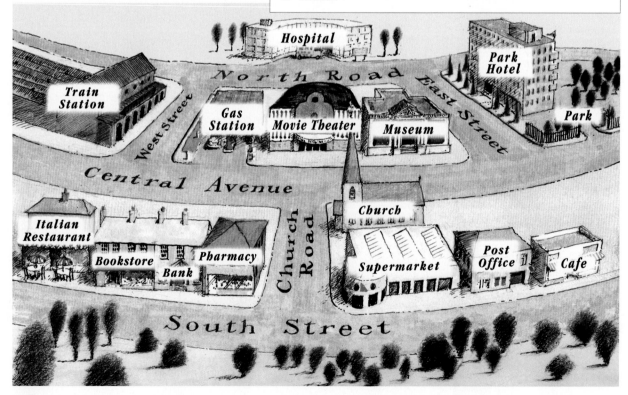

e **7.19** Listen and repeat the dialogue. Copy the rhythm and polite intonation.

f Practice in pairs. Choose places on the map.

> Excuse me. Is there a … near here?

> Yes, there's one on…

2 UNDERSTANDING & GIVING DIRECTIONS

a **7.20** Match the words and pictures. Listen and repeat.

A Turn right. **B** Turn left. **C** Go straight ahead.

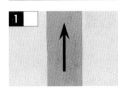 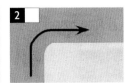 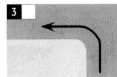

b **7.21** Listen to the dialogue. Which building (1–10) is the bus station?

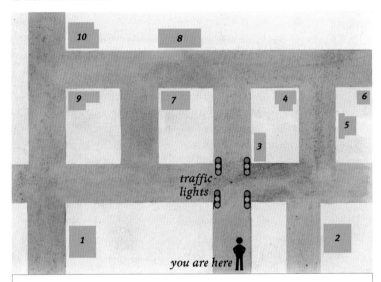

traffic lights

you are here

Tourist	Excuse me. Can you help me?
Man	Sure.
Tourist	Where's the bus station, please?
Man	Go straight ahead, and turn right. Turn right again, and it's on the left.
Tourist	Thanks very much.
Man	You're welcome.

c **7.22** Listen to two more tourists. Which building (1–10) is …?

the gas station ☐   the museum ☐

d In pairs, practice the dialogue in **b**.

e In pairs, role-play directions.

A You're going to give **B** directions to **the Park Hotel**. Choose a building 1–10. You're going to ask **B** for directions to **the hospital**. You speak first.

B You're going to ask **A** for directions to **the Park Hotel**. You speak first. You're going to give **A** directions to **the hospital**. Choose a building 1–10.

B
> Excuse me. Can you help me?
> Where's the Park Hotel, please?

A
> Go straight ahead, and then turn …

3 PEOPLE ON THE STREET 🖵

Is there a / an … near here?

a **7.23** Listen to Megan answering the question and complete the place and directions.

 Megan

1 **Place** _____
2 **Directions** "Yes. It's on the _____, _____ the coffee shop."

b **7.24** Now listen to four more people and complete the information.

 Lauren

1 **Place** _____
2 **Directions** "Yes, turn _____, it's on the right, _____ the hotel."

 Daniel

1 **Place** _____
2 **Directions** "Yes, there's one on West 61st Street, _____, the _____."

 Suzy

1 **Place** _____
2 **Directions** "Yes, there's one on London Road, _____ the _____."

 Brittany

1 **Place** _____
2 **Directions** "Yeah, it's _____."

WORDS AND PHRASES TO LEARN

Excuse me. Where's the *bank*?
Can you help me?
Is there a *gas station* near here?
   Yes, there's one on the corner.
It's be<u>tween</u> the *bank* and the *post office*.
It's <u>across</u> from the *pharmacy*.
It's next to the *bookstore*.
Go straight ahead.
Turn right / left.
It's on the right / left.

GRAMMAR

Circle the correct answer.

Hello, _____ Alex.
a I   (b) I'm

1 Are you _____ right now?
  a read   b reading
2 She's not _____ a computer.
  a using   b useing
3 They're _____ in the ocean.
  a swiming   b swimming
4 _____ get married next month.
  a She goes to   b She's going to
5 Where _____ to go next summer?
  a you are going   b are you going
6 I'm _____ to go to a university.
  a going not   b not going
7 **A** Are they going to come tonight?
  B Yes, they _____.
  a are   b 're going
8 _____ to buy a new car.
  a We're going   b We going
9 I think it's _____ be hot tomorrow.
  a going to   b going
10 _____ it going to rain?
  a Does   b Is

VOCABULARY

a Write the verb.

1 _____travel_____
2 _____
3 _____
4 _____
5 _____

b Write the next time word or phrase.

twelve, thirteen, _fourteen_

1 yesterday, today, _____
2 next Sunday, next Monday, _____
3 next week, next month, next _____

c Complete with a verb from the list.

do	get	go	meet	take

_____go_____ to work
1 _____ an e-mail
2 _____ to the gym
3 _____ outside the theater
4 _____ homework
5 _____ an umbrella
6 _____ photos
7 _____ up in the morning
8 _____ housework
9 _____ somebody for the first time
10 _____ shopping

d Complete the phrases.

Do you **p**_refer_ tea or coffee?

1 **A** Was the hotel expensive?
  B No, it was $50 a night, **i**_____ breakfast.
2 **A** When did you come back from Morocco?
  B On Sunday. We had a great **t**_____.
3 **A** Do you think it's going to be a nice day?
  B No, I think it's going to **r**_____.
4 **A** Is there a bank near here?
  B Yes, there's one **n**_____ to the museum.
5 **A** Excuse me, where's the bus station?
  B Go straight ahead, and **t**_____ left.

PRONUNCIATION

a Can you remember these words and sounds?

vowels   consonants

b ➲ p.117 / 119 **Sound Bank.** Check the words and sounds, and practice saying the example words.

c Underline the stressed syllable.

Italian

traveling	tomorrow	sunny	afternoon	across

What can you do?

1 CAN YOU UNDERSTAND THIS TEXT?

a Read the article and put an ✘ for the continent(s) Jesper <u>didn't</u> visit.

- ☐ Africa
- ☐ North America
- ☐ South America
- ☐ Asia
- ☐ Europe
- ☐ Oceania (Australia, New Zealand, etc.)
- ☐ Antarctica

I ran a marathon every day– for nearly two years!

ON JANUARY 1ST, I started my world run at 7:00 a.m. in Greenwich, London. I ran every day from about 8:00 in the morning to 4:00 or 5:00 in the afternoon, almost 45 kilometers a day (a marathon every day!). I slept in a tent or in hotels. First, I ran through Europe. In Sweden, the temperature was −11°C [12°F]. Russia

Jesper Olsen, 34, from Denmark

was difficult with a lot of snow and dangerous roads. In Siberia, people invited me into their houses for food. One night in Japan, I couldn't find my hotel because I couldn't speak Japanese. In Australia, it was summer, and the temperature was 35°C [95°F]. From Australia, I flew to the United States, and I ran north to Canada. Then I ran down the East Coast to New York. Then I went back to Europe and crossed the finish line in Greenwich on October 23rd – 22 months after I started. I was the first runner to run all around the world. 26,000 kilometers and 26 pairs of running shoes!

What's my next adventure going to be? I'm going to run from the north of Europe to South Africa, then I'm going to fly to Ushuaia in South America, and then run to North America. It's going to take two years!

Adapted from a website

b Read the article again. Answer the questions.

1. When did Jesper start his run?
2. How far did he run every day?
3. Where did he sleep?
4. Where did he have a language problem?
5. Where did he have a problem because it was very hot?
6. Where's he going to start and finish his next run?

c Look at the highlighted words and phrases and guess their meaning. Check with your teacher or a dictionary.

2 CAN YOU WRITE THIS IN ENGLISH?

Read Claudia's e-mail, and then write to her. Tell her about:

- you and your family (brothers / sisters / children)
- where you live
- what you are doing right now
- what you are going to do next summer

New Message

To:

Subject:

Hi!

My name's Claudia, and I'm from Peru. I'm a nurse. I'm married, and I have two children—a boy and a girl. We live in Arequipa, a big city in the south of Peru. It's a nice city. There are a lot of parks and many beautiful buildings.

We bought a new house in April, and right now, I'm using the computer in the bedroom. My son is watching TV with some friends, and my daughter is riding her bike. My husband is making dinner!

What are you going to do this summer? Do you have any plans? We're going to go on vacation to Mancora. It's beautiful there.

Write to me, and tell me about your life.

Best wishes,

Claudia

3 CAN YOU UNDERSTAND THESE PEOPLE?

7.25 Listen and choose the right answer.

1. What is the woman doing?
   - a Reading.
   - b Writing an e-mail.
2. The husband is _____.
   - a playing basketball
   - b watching basketball
3. Where are they going to go in the summer?
   - a To the mountains.
   - b To the beach.
4. The girl thinks the movie was _____.
   - a very good
   - b the usual
5. Tomorrow in the south it's going to _____.
   - a be cold but sunny
   - b rain
6. Where's the post office?
   - a Across from the gas station.
   - b Across from the bus station.
7. What are the directions to the bank?
   - a Go straight ahead and turn left.
   - b Go straight ahead and turn right.

4 CAN YOU SAY THIS IN ENGLISH?

Check (✔) the boxes.
Can you…?

talk about activities you are doing now	☐ Yes, I can.
tell / ask people about plans	☐ Yes, I can.
make predictions about the future	☐ Yes, I can.
give and understand simple directions	☐ Yes, I can.

START

1 spell your first name and your last name

2 count from 1–20

14 say what time you usually go to bed during the week and on the weekend

13 say what time it is now

12 ask somebody in your group a question beginning with *Where do you...?*

11 say three things people eat in your country

15 say the days of the week

16 say five things that you do on a typical day

17 say one thing you <u>can't</u> do
a) in a movie theater
b) in a museum
c) on a plane

18 ask somebody in your group a question beginning with *What time do you...?*

30 ask somebody in your group a question beginning with *Are you going to...?*

29 say two things you're going to do tomorrow

28 say what the last movie you saw was, and what you thought of it

27 say two things that were different about your town in the past (e.g., *there wasn't an airport*)

31 say two things you are doing right now

32 say two things you aren't doing right now

33 say what the weather is going to be tomorrow

34 say where there is a restaurant near the school

3 name five things in the classroom

4 say three things you have in your bag or pocket

5 say three things about someone in your family (e.g., names, age, description)

6 ask somebody in your group a question beginning with *Are you...?*

10 say what time you usually have breakfast during the week and on the weekend

9 say where you live and what you do

8 count in tens from 20–100

7 describe your (or your family's) car

19 say three things you can do in your town on a Saturday night

20 say how much these are in your country
a) a cup of coffee
b) a newspaper
c) a sandwich

21 say where you were yesterday at 6 a.m., 2 p.m., and 11 p.m.

22 say three things you did yesterday

26 say five things that are in a hotel bedroom

25 say one thing there is in your town, and one thing there isn't

24 ask somebody in your group a question beginning with *Did you...?*

23 say when your birthday is and another birthday in your family

35 say how to get to the bathrooms from your classroom (*Go out of the classroom, turn ...*)

36 ask somebody in your group a question beginning with *What do you think of...?*

FINISH

Communication

1B Guess the countries **Student A**

a Complete the information. Ask **B** about photo 1. Say *Is she from…?* Write the country under the photo.

b Answer **B**'s question about photo 2. Say *Yes, she is* or *No, she isn't.*

c Continue with the other photos.

Oksana Akinshina

She's from _____.

Adriana Fonseca

She's from Mexico.

Nanako Matsushima

She's from _____.

Imanol Arias

He's from Spain.

Ricky Gervais

He's from _____.

Stephen Chow

He's from China.

Maria Grazia Cucinotta

She's from _____.

Jennifer Hudson

She's from the US.

PE 1 Game: Hit the ships **Student A**

a Draw 5 "ships" in **Your ships**.
1 ship = three squares

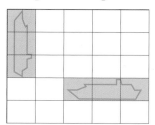

Your ships

	11	12	13	14	15	16	17	18	19	20
A										
B										
C										
D										
E										
F										
G										
H										
I										
J										

B's ships

	11	12	13	14	15	16	17	18	19	20
A										
B										
C										
D										
E										
F										
G										
H										
I										
J										

b Try to "hit" **B**'s ships. Say a square, e.g., H16. If **B** says *hit*, check (✔) the square in **B's ships**. If **B** says *nothing*, put an ✘ in the square.

c **B** says a square. Say *hit* or *nothing*.

PE 2 Personal information **Student A**

a Interview **B** and complete **B**'s form.

> **B**
> First name ＿＿＿ Last name ＿＿＿
> Nationality ＿＿＿
> Address ＿＿＿
> Zip code ＿＿＿
> Age ＿＿＿
> Married ☐ Single ☐
> Phone number: home ＿＿＿
> ⠀⠀⠀⠀⠀⠀⠀⠀⠀⠀⠀ cell ＿＿＿
> E-mail address ＿＿＿

> ⚠ **E-mail addresses**
> @ = at
> . = dot

b Answer **B**'s questions. Use the information in the **YOU** form.

> **YOU**
> First name _Alex_ Last name _Barrett_
> Nationality _British_
> Address _15 Parkhill Road, Columbus, Ohio_
> Zip code _43085_
> Age _25_
> Married ☐ Single ✔
> Phone number: home _780-2344_
> ⠀⠀⠀⠀⠀⠀⠀⠀⠀⠀⠀ cell _614 555-6943_
> E-mail address _abarrett@btalk.com_

PE 3 *What time is it?* **Student A**

Ask **B** questions to complete the times on the clocks.

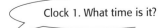
Clock 1. What time is it?

5A *Where were they?* **Student A**

a Ask **B** your questions.

1 Where was Sting? (He was at the movies.)
2 Where was Barbra Streisand? (She was on a plane.)
3 Where was Morgan Freeman? (He was in bed.)
4 Where was Jennifer Aniston? (She was at a restaurant.)
5 Where was Calista Flockhart? (She was in a car.)

b Answer **B**'s questions.

6A *Is there a TV? Where is it?* **Student A**

a Ask **B** questions about the things below for picture 1.

- Ask *Is there a…?* or *Are there any…?*

laptop	lamp	sodas	coat	TV	magazines
books	suitcase	towels	keys		

- If **B** answers *Yes*, ask *Where is it?* or *Where are they?* Draw the thing(s) in the right places in picture 1.

b Answer **B**'s questions about picture 2.

Communication

6B Good or bad vacation? Student A

a You went on vacation and you stayed at the Ocean View Hotel. You had a very good time. Read the information about the hotel.

> **Ocean View Hotel** **** **$75 a night**
> swimming pool ✔ (and a children's pool)
> restaurants ✔ (two, very good)
> a spa ✔ (fantastic)
> a gym ✘
> beach ✔ (very beautiful)

b Look at the questions. What words are missing?

/ you have a good time?
Where / you stay?
/ there a swimming pool?
/ there a good restaurant?
/ there a spa?
/ there a gym?
/ there a nice beach?
/ it expensive?

c **B** asks you about your vacation. Answer the questions.

d **B** went on vacation last week, too. Ask him / her the questions.

> Did you have a good time?

> Was there a...?

1B Guess the countries Student B

a Answer **A**'s question about photo 1. Say *Yes, she is* or *No, she isn't*.

b Complete the information. Ask **A** about photo 2. Say *Is she from…?* Write the country under the photo.

c Continue with the other photos.

1 Oksana Akinshina

She's from Russia.

2 Adriana Fonseca

She's from _____.

3 Nanako Matsushima

She's from Japan.

4 Imanol Arias

He's from _____.

5 Ricky Gervais

He's from England.

6 Stephen Chow

He's from _____.

7 Maria Grazia Cucinotta

She's from Italy.

8 Jennifer Hudson

She's from _____.

PE 1 Game: Hit the ships **Student B**

a Draw 5 "ships" in **Your ships**. 1 ship = three squares

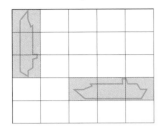

Your ships

	11	12	13	14	15	16	17	18	19	20
A										
B										
C										
D										
E										
F										
G										
H										
I										
J										

A's ships

	11	12	13	14	15	16	17	18	19	20
A										
B										
C										
D										
E										
F										
G										
H										
I										
J										

b **A** says a square, e.g., H16. If you have a ship in H16, say *hit*. If not, say *nothing*.

c Try to "hit" **A**'s ships. Say a square, e.g., B12. If **A** says *hit*, check (✔) the square in **A's ships**. If **A** says *nothing*, put an ✘ in the square.

PE 2 Personal information **Student B**

a Answer **A**'s questions. Use the information in the **YOU** form.

> **YOU**
> First name *Chris* Last name *Lennox*
> Nationality *American*
> Address *81 West Street, Gainesville, Florida*
> Zip code *32601*
> Age *31*
> Married ✔ Single ☐
> Phone number: home *342-7152*
>   cell *352 555-5661*
> E-mail address chris@mac.com

> ⚠ **E-mail addresses**
>   @ = *at*
>   . = *dot*

b Interview **A** and complete **A**'s form.

> **A**
> First name _____ Last name _____
> Nationality _____
> Address _____
> Zip code _____
> Age _____
> Married ☐ Single ☐
> Phone number: home _____
>   cell _____
> E-mail address _____

PE 3 *What time is it?* **Student B**

Ask **A** questions to complete the times on the clocks.

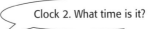

Clock 2. What time is it?

Communication

5A *Where were they?* **Student B**

a Answer **A**'s questions.

b Ask **A** your questions.

1 Where was Danny DeVito? (He was at the hairdresser.)
2 Where was Lucy Liu? (She was on a bus.)
3 Where was James Blunt? (He was in a meeting.)
4 Where was Tina Turner? (She was in the park.)
5 Where was Jack Nicholson? (He was at the gym.)

6A *Is there a TV? Where is it?* **Student B**

a Answer **A**'s questions about picture 1.

b Ask **A** questions about the things below for picture 2.

• Ask *Is there a...?* or *Are there any...?*

TV	extra pillows	sodas	towels	remote control
books	laptop	clock	bag	pens

• If **A** answers *Yes*, ask *Where is it?* or *Where are they?*
  Draw the thing(s) in the right places in picture 2.

6B *Good or bad vacation?* **Student B**

a You went on vacation and you stayed at the Palace Hotel. You had a terrible time! Read the information about the hotel.

> **Palace Hotel** **** **$300 a night**
> swimming pool ✔ (but very small)
> restaurants ✔ (one, food was very bad,
>   service was very slow)
> a spa ✗
> a gym ✔ (but closed!)
> beach ✔ (10 miles from the hotel)

b Look at the questions. What words are missing?

/ you have a good time?
Where / you stay?
/ there a swimming pool?
/ there a good restaurant?
/ there a spa?
/ there a gym?
/ there a nice beach?
/ it expensive?

c **A** went on vacation last week. Ask him / her the questions.

> Did you have a good time?
>
> Was there a...?

d **A** asks you about your vacation. Answer the questions.

2A Memory game **Students A + B**

a Look at the photo for 30 seconds.

b Close your book. In pairs, can you remember all the things on the table?

3A A new haircut
Students A + B

7C Students A + B

Audioscripts

1.8

1, 2,… 3
7, 8,… 9
6, 5,… 4
6, 7,… 8
3, 2,… 1
9, 8,… 7
4, 3,… 2
8, 9,… 10
3, 4,… 5
2, 1,… zero

1.12

1 Where is it? Turkey.
2 Where is it? Mexico.
3 Where is it? Japan.
4 Where is it? Italy.

1.15

Woman Where's he from?
Man He's from the United States.
Woman Is she from the United States, too?
Man No, she isn't. She's from England.
Woman Is it a good movie?
Man Yes, it is. It's great.

1.18

1 Is she from Brazil? No, she isn't.
2 It's from China.
3 She's from Japan.
4 Is he from Turkey? Yes, he is.
5 He's from the United States.
6 Is she from Mexico? No, she isn't.
7 She's from England.
8 Where's he from? He's from Peru.

1.23

1 Is she from Italy?
2 He's from Russia.
3 Where's he from?
4 It's from Korea.
5 She's late.
6 Where is he?

1.25

1 I'm from Brazil.
  She's Brazilian.
2 I'm from Spain.
  He's Spanish.
3 I'm from Russia.
  She's Russian.
4 I'm from the United States.
  He's American.
5 I'm from Mexico.
  He's Mexican.
6 I'm from Italy.
  She's Italian.
7 I'm from Korea.
  She's Korean.
8 I'm from Japan.
  She's Japanese.
9 I'm from England.
  He's English.

10 I'm from China.
   He's Chinese.
11 I'm from Peru.
   She's Peruvian.
12 I'm from Turkey.
   He's Turkish.

1.29

1 I'm Peruvian.
  I'm not Peruvian.
2 They're Japanese.
  They aren't Japanese.
3 She's Brazilian.
  She isn't Brazilian.
4 We're English.
  We aren't English.
5 It's Italian.
  It isn't Italian.
6 You're American.
  You aren't American.
7 He's Russian.
  He isn't Russian.

1.33

A He's American. He's number twelve.
B He's English. He's number eleven.

1.35

1
Passengers on Flight KLM 9246 to Miami,
  please go to gate B14.
This is the final call for passengers on Flight
  KLM 9246 to Miami. Please go to gate B14
  immediately.
Mr. Pablo Torres on flight KLM 9246 to
  Miami, please go to gate B14 immediately.

2
Receptionist Good morning.
Man Hello. I'm Pablo Torres. I have a reservation.
Receptionist How do you spell your last name?
Man T-O-R-R-E-S.
Receptionist Excuse me?
Man T-O-R-R-E-S.
Receptionist Thank you.

1.40

1 N
2 Q
3 J
4 E
5 Y
6 W
7 B
8 A

1.41

1 DJ
2 BMW
3 TV
4 PC
5 CD
6 DVD

1.43

Interviewer What's your name?
Man Michael.

1.44

Interviewer How do you spell it?
Man M-I-C-H-A-E-L.

1.45

Interviewer Where are you from?
Man Queens, New York.

1.46

Interviewer What's your name?
Speaker 1 My name is Linda.
Interviewer How do you spell it?
Speaker 1 L-I-N-D-A.
Interviewer Where are you from?
Speaker 1 I'm from Los Angeles, California.

Interviewer What's your name?
Speaker 2 My name's Sarah.
Interviewer How do you spell it?
Speaker 2 S-A-R-A-H.
Interviewer Where are you from?
Speaker 1 I'm from Reading, in England.

Interviewer What's your name?
Speaker 3 My name is Joshua.
Interviewer How do you spell it?
Speaker 3 J-O-S-H-U-A.
Interviewer Where are you from?
Speaker 3 I'm from Chicago, in the United
  States of America.

Interviewer What's your name?
Speaker 4 Elena.
Interviewer How do you spell it?
Speaker 4 E-L-E-N-A.
Interviewer Where are you from?
Speaker 4 Brazil.

Interviewer What's your name?
Speaker 5 Padma.
Interviewer How do you spell it?
Speaker 5 P-A-D-M-A.
Interviewer Where are you from?
Speaker 5 I'm from Bangalore, India.

Interviewer What's your name?
Speaker 6 My name's Tom.
Interviewer How do you spell it?
Speaker 6 T-O-M.
Interviewer Where are you from?
Speaker 6 I'm from Vancouver, in Canada.

1.48

1 Look at the board, please.
2 Open your books.
3 Go to page 14.
4 Stand up.
5 Sit down, please.
6 Close the door.

1.49

Stand up.
Sit down, please.
Open your books.
Go to page 12.
Look at exercise 1b.
Look at the board.
Close your books.

2.6

It's a photo… They're photos.
It's a class… They're classes.
It's a key… They're keys.
It's a door… They're doors.
It's a phone… They're phones.
It's a watch… They're watches.
It's a dictionary… They're dictionaries.
It's a table… They're tables.
It's a book… They're books.
It's a pen… They're pens.

2.7

1 **A** Is this your bag?
　B Oh! Yes, it is! Thank you.
2 **A** Good afternoon.
　B Hello. We're Paul Jones and Martin Smith.
　　We have reservations.
　A Let's see… Yes. Rooms 625 and 626.
　　Here are your keys.
　B Thank you.
　C Thanks.
3 **A** What's that music?
　B Sorry, it's my cell phone. Oh, hi, Andy.
4 **A** Excuse me, what's this word?
　B Look in the dictionary.
5 **A** How much is it?
　B Twenty dollars.
　A Is a credit card OK?
　B Yes, of course.

2.15

1 Miranda is Carrie's friend.
2 Pam is Bridget's mother.
3 Captain Teague is Jack Sparrow's father.
4 Leia is Luke's sister.
5 Prince Philip is the Queen's husband.

2.17

1 It's American.
2 It's French.
3 It's British.
4 It's Japanese.
5 It's German.
6 It's Italian.

2.27

1
Sam Hello, Mike.
Mike Hi, Sam. How are you?
Sam Fine, thanks. And you?
Mike I'm OK, thanks. This is Helen. She's a
　friend from work.
Sam Nice to meet you.
Woman Hi.
Mike Sorry, we're in a hurry. See you soon. Bye.
Sam Bye.

2
Girl 1 Look. This is my brother.
Girl 2 Wow! He's very good-looking. What's
　his name?
Girl 1 Adam.
Girl 2 Is he married?
Girl 1 No, he isn't.
Girl 2 How old is he?
Girl 1 He's twenty-six.
Girl 2 What's his cell phone number?

2.29

A What's your phone number?
B 207 555-8962.
A Excuse me?
B 207 555-8962.

2.33

1　13
2　40
3　50
4　16
5　70
6　18
7　19

2.34

Interviewer Do you have brothers and sisters?
Matthew I have one brother and one sister.

2.35

Interviewer How old are they?
Matthew My sister is 23, and my brother is 17.

2.36

Interviewer Do you have brothers and sisters?
Elena Yes, I have one brother.
Interviewer How old is he?
Elena 25 years old.

Interviewer Do you have brothers and sisters?
Hampton I have one sister.
Interviewer How old is she?
Hampton She's 13.

Interviewer Do you have brothers and sisters?
Jared Yes, I have one brother and one sister.
Interviewer How old are they?
Jared My brother's 22. My sister's 26.

Interviewer Do you have brothers and sisters?
Lauren I have one brother.
Interviewer How old is he?
Lauren He is 17 years old.

Interviewer Do you have brothers and sisters?
Sohail Yes, I have three sisters.
Interviewer How old are they?
Sohail 36, 28, and 39.

Interviewer Do you have brothers and sisters?
Anna I have four brothers.
Interviewer How old are they?
Anna 46, 44, 43, and 36.

3.1

Hairdresser Hello. Is this your first time here?
Woman Yes, it is.
Hairdresser Do you live near here?
Woman No, I don't. I live downtown.
Hairdresser Oh, nice. How do you want your
　hair?
Woman I don't know. Something different.
Hairdresser Do you want a coffee?
Woman No, thanks. I don't drink coffee.
Hairdresser Do you want a magazine?
Woman Yes, please. Oh, look. Demi Moore's
　children.
Hairdresser Do you have children?
Woman Yes, I do. I have two boys.
Hairdresser How old are they?
Woman Eight and ten.
***
Woman It's very short.
Hairdresser Don't worry. Wait.
***
Hairdresser OK. Do you like it?

3.6

Taxi driver Good morning! Where to?
Woman Geary Street, please.
Taxi driver OK. The traffic is bad this
　morning.
Woman Yes. It's terrible.
Taxi driver Do you live in San Francisco?
Woman Yes, I do.
Taxi driver Are you OK? What's the problem?
Woman I don't like my new haircut.
Taxi driver Why not? I like it.
Woman Really? Do you like it?
Taxi driver Yes, I do.
Woman Thanks.
Taxi driver Where do you want to stop?
Woman Over there, at Macy's. I want a new bag.
Taxi driver OK. That's 14.50.
Woman Here's 16. Keep the change.
Taxi driver Thanks very much! Have a nice day.

3.11

Interviewer What do you usually have for
　breakfast?
William I usually have cereal and tea.
Interviewer Not coffee?
William No, I prefer tea. Not very American,
　I know!
Interviewer Isn't a typical American breakfast
　eggs, potatoes, sausage, and toast?
William Yes, but I only have that on the
　weekend.
Interviewer What do you have for lunch?
William I have a sandwich at work, in my
　office, and juice or water.
Interviewer Do you have dinner at home?
William Yes, with my family.
Interviewer What do you usually have?
William We usually have pasta or fish with
　vegetables, or maybe a salad. It depends.
Interviewer What's your favorite meal,
　breakfast, lunch, or dinner?
William Breakfast on the weekend!

Audioscripts

3.19

1 I like art. He… He likes art.
2 I speak English. She… She speaks English.
3 I live in Tokyo. My brother… My brother lives in Tokyo.
4 I watch MTV. She… She watches MTV.
5 I want a coffee. He… He wants a coffee.
6 I have a dog. John… John has a dog.
7 I don't eat meat. My sister… My sister doesn't eat meat.
8 I don't read magazines. My son… My son doesn't read magazines.
9 Do you work? He… Does he work?
10 Do you drink tea? She… Does she drink tea?

3.28

1 It's nine o'clock.
2 It's twenty after three.
3 It's nine thirty.
4 It's ten to ten.
5 It's quarter after nine.
6 It's twenty-five to twelve.
7 It's five after eight.
8 It's quarter to six.

3.29

Interviewer What do you do?
Christian I'm a salesperson.

3.30

Interviewer Do you like it?
Christian Yes.

3.31

Interviewer What time do you start and finish?
Christian I start at 7 a.m. in the morning, and I finish at 7:30 p.m. in the evening.

3.32

Interviewer What do you do?
Megan I am a teacher.
Interviewer Do you like it?
Megan I like my job.
Interviewer What time do you start and finish?
Megan I start work at nine o'clock. I finish work at four o'clock.

Interviewer What do you do?
Pamela I'm a nurse.
Interviewer Do you like it?
Pamela Of course.
Interviewer What time do you start and finish?
Pamela I work nine to four.

Interviewer What do you do?
Chris I'm a factory worker.
Interviewer Do you like it?
Chris No, no, I don't.
Interviewer What time do you start and finish?
Chris I start at six in the morning and finish at two in the afternoon.

Interviewer What do you do?
Daniel I'm a lawyer.
Interviewer Do you like it?
Daniel I do.
Interviewer What time do you start and finish?
Daniel It varies, but I usually start work at about nine in the morning, and I usually finish at around six in the evening.

3.34

1 **A** What day is it today?
  B It's Tuesday. Why?
  A Because it's my wife's birthday on Friday, and I don't have a present!
2 **A** Is tomorrow Wednesday?
  B No, Thursday. Today is Wednesday.

4.1

Interviewer What time do you get up?
Anna Very early! At six o'clock.
Interviewer Do you take a shower?
Anna Yes.
Interviewer What do you have for breakfast?
Anna Fruit or cereal. And coffee.
Interviewer Do you have breakfast sitting down or standing up?
Anna Sitting down.
Interviewer What time do you go to work?
Anna At seven. I start work at eight, but my office isn't near where I live.
Interviewer Are you in a hurry in the morning?
Anna No, because I get up at six! I have time for everything.
Interviewer Do you like mornings?
Anna Yes, I do. I like my job. I don't get up and think, "Oh, no! Work …"

4.7

Narrator Hammerfest is a small town in the north of Norway. It is near the Arctic Circle. Only 9,407 people live here. In the winter, it is light for only two or three hours. People have breakfast, lunch, and dinner in the dark. In the summer, it is light for 24 hours, and people go to bed very late. Some people play golf in the midnight sun!
  Knut-Arne Iversen is from Hammerfest. He works for the Tourist Information Office.

Interviewer Do a lot of tourists come to Hammerfest?
Knut-Arne Yes, about 175,000 a year.
Interviewer When do they usually come?
Knut-Arne In the summer. We don't have a lot of tourists in the winter!
Interviewer Is the winter very cold?
Knut-Arne No, not very, about -3 degrees. But we sometimes have a lot of snow, and the streets and schools are closed.
Interviewer What do people do in the winter?
Knut-Arne We play a lot of sports. We ski a lot, and we have snowmobiles. Children usually play outside, but if it's very cold, they play inside on their computer or watch TV. In the evening, we usually stay at home and relax or go and see friends. But the winter is difficult for old people.

Interviewer What do people do in the summer?
Knut-Arne Life is completely different. It's light for 24 hours a day, and the weather is sometimes very hot. People are outside all the time. We fish, and walk, and have barbecues. We don't swim because the water is very cold – maybe only 10 degrees. People don't sleep a lot, and young children say, "I don't want to go to bed. It isn't dark."
Interviewer Do you prefer the summer or the winter?
Knut-Arne In the winter, it's nice to be at home with your family and friends, but I prefer the summer.
Interviewer Do you like life in Hammerfest?
Knut-Arne Yes. Life here is easy. It's quiet and beautiful, and the air is clean. But the winter is very long, and the summer is very short. I'm not sure if I will stay here forever.

4.16

1 We can park here.
2 I can't help you.
3 We can't stop here.
4 You can't sit here.
5 Mark can go with me.
6 I can walk home.
7 We can't come tonight.
8 You can write in the book.

4.19

1 twelve pounds seventy-five
2 fifteen dollars and ninety-nine cents
3 fifty euros ninety-nine
4 a hundred and twenty pounds
5 thirteen dollars and twenty-five cents
6 three euros twenty
7 sixty p
8 eighty cents

4.20

1
A The *New York Times*, please.
B Here you are.
A How much is it?
B It's one dollar and twenty-five cents.

2
A Can I have a phone card, please?
B For how much?
A Fifteen pounds, please.
B Here you are.
A Thanks.

3
A Can I have a memory card, please?
B Four gig or eight?
A Four, please. How much is it?
B Four ninety-nine.
A Can I pay with MasterCard?
B Sure.

4
A A ticket to Paris, please.
B One-way or round trip?
A Uh, round trip.
B Thirty euros twenty.
A Oh! OK.

4.23

Man Can I help you?
Woman Yes, can I have a coffee and a chocolate brownie, please?
Man Espresso, Americano, or cappuccino?
Woman An espresso, please.
Man Single or double?
Woman Single. How much is it?
Man Two dollars and forty-five cents.
Woman Here you are.
Man Thanks.

4.25

Interviewer Where do you usually have lunch?
Brandy In my office.

4.26

Interviewer What do you have?
Brandy Salad.

4.27

Interviewer How much is it?
Brandy $4.

4.28

Interviewer Where do you usually have lunch?
Bridget I have lunch in my office.
Interviewer What do you have?
Bridget I have a sandwich.
Interviewer How much is it?
Bridget 2.75.

Interviewer Where do you usually have lunch?
Michael Pizza store.
Interviewer What do you have?
Michael Pizza, salad.
Interviewer How much is it?
Michael About $8.

Interviewer Where do you usually have lunch?
Helen I usually have lunch in a cafe.
Interviewer What do you have?
Helen I have a sandwich and some fruit.
Interviewer How much is it?
Helen It's about £2.70.

Interviewer Where do you usually have lunch?
Dax Usually at a restaurant near my house.
Interviewer What do you have?
Dax Usually chicken, rice, and beans.
Interviewer How much is it?
Dax About $7.

5.5

1 He's a teacher.
  He was a teacher.
2 Is she at school?
  Was she at school?
3 They aren't happy.
  They weren't happy.
4 It isn't cold.
  It wasn't cold.
5 We're late.
  We were late.

6 Are you tired?
  Were you tired?
7 I'm very hungry.
  I was very hungry.
8 You aren't at home.
  You weren't at home.

5.8

Linda Hello.
Ben Hi, honey.
Linda Oh, hi, Dad. How's Paris?
Ben Fine. A lot of work. Did you have a good day?
Linda It was OK.
Ben What did you do?
Linda I got up early. I went to school.
Ben How was it?
Linda Great! We didn't have classes. We went to an art museum.
Ben Oh, nice. Did you have lunch there?
Linda Yes, we had lunch at the cafe. And then I went shopping with Katy.
Ben Did you do your homework?
Linda Yes, of course. I always do my homework.
Ben Who's that, Linda?

5.9

Ben Who's that, Linda?
Linda What?
Ben I can hear somebody.
Linda Oh, it's just the TV.
Ben Can I speak to your mother?
Linda Mom? She's out. She went to the movies with her friends.
Ben Are you alone?
Linda Yes. I am.
Ben Linda, is somebody with you?
Linda Uh…Yes, Dad. Annie, Sophie, and Tony are here.
Ben Oh. Who are they? And who's Tony?
Linda He's a friend, Dad. He's very nice, and Sophie and Annie are too.

5.10

What do you do?
  What did you do?
I get up early.
  I got up early.
We don't have classes.
  We didn't have classes.
We go to an art museum.
  We went to an art museum.
We have lunch at the cafe.
  We had lunch at the cafe.

5.12

1 What time did you get up?
2 Did you have breakfast? What did you have?
3 Did you go to work?
4 Where did you have lunch? What did you have?
5 Did you go to the gym?
6 Did you go shopping?
7 Did you have dinner at home? What did you have?
8 Did you watch TV? What did you watch?
9 What time did you go to bed?

5.14 and **5.17**

1 I went to the airport with my mother.
2 My friends went to the airport, too.
3 They helped me with my suitcases.
4 It was early. We waited at check-in.
5 I kissed my mother good-bye.
6 My mother cried.
7 My friends were sad, too. They wanted to come.
8 I arrived in Rome at 11 o'clock.

5.19

1 stay	stayed
2 buy	bought
3 rent	rented
4 say	said
5 like	liked
6 speak	spoke
7 can / can't	could / couldn't
8 start	started
9 make	made
10 find	found
11 learn	learned
12 change	changed
13 live	lived
14 meet	met
15 break	broke
16 come back	came back

5.22

one… the first
two… the second
five… the fifth
eighteen… the eighteenth
eleven… the eleventh
three… the third
twenty… the twentieth
nine… the ninth
twenty-one… the twenty-first
twenty-four… the twenty-fourth
thirty… the thirtieth

5.24

1
Man What's the date today?
Woman It's May fifth.
Man It is? I thought it was the fourth.

2
Woman When's your birthday?
Man July twentieth.

5.26

Interviewer When's your birthday?
Corinne My birthday is October 1st.

5.27

Interviewer What did you do on your last birthday?
Corinne On my last birthday, I had a lot of food.

Audioscripts

5.28

Interviewer When's your birthday?
Joshua May 4th.
Interviewer What did you do on your last birthday?
Joshua I went to a club, and I had dinner.

Interviewer When's your birthday?
Hampton January 28th.
Interviewer What did you do on your last birthday?
Hampton I saw a movie.

Interviewer When's your birthday?
Christian August 5th.
Interviewer What did you do on your last birthday?
Christian I can't remember.

Interviewer When's your birthday?
Laura My birthday is July 11th.
Interviewer What did you do on your last birthday?
Laura I had a party with some friends.

6.3

Man Hello. We have a reservation.
Receptionist Let's see, yes, Mr. and Mrs. Robson. Welcome to the island. Your room's upstairs, number seven.
Woman Is there an elevator?
Receptionist No, I'm sorry, there isn't. But I can help you with your suitcases.

***

Receptionist This is your room.
Woman It's very small.
Receptionist Yes, but there's a beautiful view.
Man There are two beds. We wanted a double bed.
Receptionist I'm sorry, there aren't any rooms with a double bed.
Woman Where's the TV?
Receptionist There isn't one. There are some books over there.
Woman Books!
Receptionist This is the bathroom.
Woman There isn't a bathtub.
Receptionist No, there's a shower. It uses less water.
Man Can I use the Internet here?
Receptionist No, I'm sorry you can't.
Woman Are there any stores near here?
Receptionist No, ma'am, there aren't. Enjoy your stay.

6.5

Woman We don't like the room, and we don't like the hotel.
Man We want to go back home. When's the next boat?
Receptionist I'm very sorry, sir. There's only one boat a day in the winter – and it left five minutes ago. There isn't another boat until tomorrow afternoon.
Woman 24 hours here! There isn't a TV. There aren't any stores. What can we do?

6.8

Interviewer Mr. Soriano, what differences are there between Benidorm today and Benidorm in the 1950s?
Mr. Soriano There are very big differences. For example, today, there are 65,000 people who live in Benidorm. In the 1950s, there were only about 3,000 people.
Interviewer Wow! That's a big difference! What about tourists?
Mr. Soriano Today there are four million tourists a year. In the 1950s, there were only maybe 300 tourists. And they were Spanish. Now tourists come from all over the world.
Interviewer Was there an airport near Benidorm in the 1950s?
Mr. Soriano No, there wasn't an airport then. Today there is a big international airport in Alicante, which is only 35 miles from Benidorm.
Interviewer How many hotels are there now?
Mr. Soriano There are 128 hotels in the town.
Interviewer That's a lot! And in the 1950s?
Mr. Soriano In the 1950s, there were only three. And there wasn't a supermarket in the 1950s, only some little stores. Today there are 264 supermarkets and hundreds of stores.
Interviewer Thank you, Mr. Soriano.
Mr. Soriano You're welcome.

6.12

English friend How was your weekend, Kelly? What did you do?
Kelly We went to Blackpool.
English friend Blackpool? Why Blackpool?
Kelly Well, somebody told us that Blackpool was like Benidorm… in Spain. Well, maybe it is in the summer, but it certainly isn't in April. The weather was terrible! And a lot of places were closed, you know the restaurants and cafes. There was nothing to do.
English friend Where did you stay? In a hotel?
Kelly I wanted to stay in a good hotel, but Jeff wanted something typically English so we stayed in a bed and breakfast.
English friend How was it?
Kelly Well, the room was really small. And the breakfast was terrible!
English friend Terrible? English breakfasts are usually very good!
Kelly Yes, and that's what we wanted, a typical English breakfast, you know, eggs, sausage, and toast. But there was only cereal, cold bread, and tea. There wasn't any coffee! The weekend was a complete disaster.

6.15

Narrator I opened the door of my apartment and turned on the light. Oh, no! My apartment looked very different. There was no TV, no radio. There weren't any pictures on the walls. I went into my bedroom. My laptop wasn't there! But there was a nice smell. Chanel Number 5.

6.16

see	saw
leave	left
think	thought
drink	drank
tell	told
drive	drove
give	gave
read	read
send	sent

6.19

1 Did you see the movie? Yes, I saw it yesterday.
2 Did you buy the books? Yes, I bought them yesterday.
3 Did you meet Ana? Yes, I met her yesterday.
4 Did John call you? Yes, he called me yesterday.
5 Did Silvia tell you about the party? Yes, she told us yesterday.

6.25

Interviewer What's the last movie you saw?
Lauren I saw *The Visitor*.

6.26

Interviewer What did you think of it?
Lauren I thought it was great.

6.27

Interviewer What's the last movie you saw?
Dax *WALL•E*.
Interviewer What did you think of it?
Dax I liked it a lot. It was really interesting.

Interviewer What's the last movie you saw?
Paul I saw the new *Indiana Jones* movie.
Interviewer What did you think of it?
Paul It was OK.

Interviewer What's the last movie you saw?
Corinne Oh, the last movie I saw was *Mamma Mia!*
Interviewer What did you think of it?
Corinne I liked it. I thought it was very good.

Interviewer What's the last movie you saw?
Anna *Lars and the Real Girl.*
Interviewer What did you think of it?
Anna It was fantastic.

Interviewer What's the last movie you saw?
Joshua I saw *Wanted* with Angelina Jolie.
Interviewer What did you think of it?
Joshua I thought it was terrible.

7.1

Host OK, David and Kim. You have one minute. What are they doing?
David Is it a man or a woman?
Kim It's a woman. Look at her hair. What's she doing?
David Is she playing the piano?
Kim No, she isn't. She's using a computer.
David Yes, OK. I think you're right. And the next one?

Kim It's a man and a woman. They're eating pasta.

David No, they aren't eating pasta. They're eating Chinese food.

Host Time's up, Kim and David. Are those your answers?

David Yes, they are.

Host OK. So what do you think? Are they right or wrong?

7.2

Host OK. So what do you think? Are they right or wrong?

Audience Right! Wrong!

Host Let's see. Number one. And… They're right! She's using a computer. What about number two? Are they eating Chinese food? Sorry, Kim and David, you're wrong. They're eating pasta. Kim was right the first time.

7.6

Jerry What exactly are your plans, Liz?

Liz I'm going to ride a bike from Ecuador to Argentina.

Jerry Wow! How far is that?

Liz It's about 4,700 miles.

Jerry Are you going to go alone?

Liz No, I'm not. I'm going to go with a friend.

Jerry Where are you going to stay?

Liz We're going to camp, and maybe sometimes stay in small hotels.

Jerry When are you going to start your trip?

Liz In October. And we aren't going to come back until April.

Jerry Six months – that's a long time! Are you excited?

Liz Yes, I am. It's going to be a great trip!

7.10

go to work… I'm going to go to work tomorrow.

watch TV… I'm going to watch TV tomorrow.

get up early… I'm going to get up early tomorrow.

go shopping… I'm going to go shopping tomorrow.

make lunch… I'm going to make lunch tomorrow.

come to class… I'm going to come to class tomorrow.

go to the gym… I'm going to go to the gym tomorrow.

see my friends… I'm going to see my friends tomorrow.

7.11

Jerry So, how was the trip, Liz?

Liz It was great, fantastic! We had a great time!

Jerry Did you ride your bikes to the South of Argentina?

Liz Yes, we did. 4,700 miles.

Jerry Wow! That's amazing. And did you ride all the way?

Liz Almost. One day in Chile we took a bus, because I was sick, and I couldn't ride my bike.

Jerry Did you camp?

Liz We camped in Ecuador and Peru, and we sometimes stayed in small hotels. In Chile and Argentina we usually camped.

Jerry Did you have any problems?

Liz Not big problems, no. We had one problem with a bike.

Jerry What happened?

Liz Well, my friend's bike broke.

Jerry Where were you when it broke?

Liz We were near La Paz, in Bolivia.

Jerry What did you do?

Liz We were very lucky. A Bolivian man stopped to help us. He took us to La Paz in his car. We took the bike to a mechanic there, and he repaired it.

Jerry What was your favorite place?

Liz We loved all the countries we visited. The people were wonderful. But my favorite place was probably Patagonia, in the South of Argentina and Chile. It was very beautiful.

Jerry Do you have any plans for your next trip?

Liz Yes, we're going to ride bikes around India.

7.12

Female broadcaster And here's Mark with the weather.

Mark Well, tomorrow is going to be very cold here in Chicago, about 10 degrees Fahrenheit, and it's probably going to snow. Wear warm clothes!

Female broadcaster What about the rest of the country, Mark?

Mark It's also going to be cold on the East Coast, but it's not going to snow. It's going to rain in New York all day. Take an umbrella! In the southern states, the weather's going to be very different. In Miami, it's going to be very sunny and hot—up to 88 degrees! Great for the beach. On the West Coast, it's also going to be sunny, but not hot. If you live in San Francisco, you need sunglasses and a coat. But not a warm coat. It's not going to be hot, but it's not going to be cold either. So, I hope you all have a good day!

7.14

train	/eɪ/	make	play	rain
egg	/ɛ/	get	rent	send
boot	/u/	do	lose	use
phone	/oʊ/	go	know	snow
cat	/æ/	camp	have	relax
tree	/i/	meet	see	speak

7.17

1 It's across from the theater. (the movie theater)
2 It's between the school and the supermarket. (the post office)
3 It's next to the museum and across from the school. (the park)
4 It's on the corner, across from the church, and next to the post office. (the supermarket)
5 It's between the bookstore and the movie theater. (the pharmacy)
6 It's next to the music store, across from the movie theater. (the theater)
7 It's on the corner, across from the bookstore and next to the music store. (the bank)
8 It's across from the park. (the school)

7.18

A Excuse me. Is there a bank near here?

B Yes, there's one on South Street, next to the bookstore.

A Thanks.

7.20

1 Go straight ahead.
2 Turn right.
3 Turn left.

7.22

1

Tourist Excuse me! Is there a gas station near here?

Man A gas station? Let me think. Yes, I know. Go straight ahead, and turn right.

Tourist Go straight, and turn right?

Man Yes, straight ahead, and turn right. Then go straight ahead about 100 yards and turn left.

Tourist Turn left?

Man Yes, and the gas station is on the right. You can't miss it.

Tourist Thank you.

Man No problem.

2

Tourist Excuse me. Where's the museum?

Woman I'm sorry. I don't know. I don't live here.

***

Tourist Oh, excuse me. Is the museum near here?

Man 1 Sorry. No speak English.

Tourist OK, no problem.

***

Tourist Excuse me. Can you help me? I want to go to the museum.

Man 2 The museum?

Tourist Yes. Do you know where it is?

Man 2 Sure. Go straight down this street, and turn left. Then turn right and go straight ahead. Then turn left, and the museum is on the right. It's on the corner.

Tourist Thank you very much.

Man 2 Excuse me!

Tourist Yeah?

Man 2 It's closed on Mondays.

Tourist Oh, no…

7.23

Interviewer Is there a post office near here?

Megan Yes. It's on the corner, next to the coffee shop.

7.24

Interviewer Is there a coffee shop near here?

Lauren Yes. Turn right, it's on the right, next to the hotel.

Interviewer Is there a bank near here?

Daniel Yes, there's one on West 61st Street, next to the restaurant.

Interviewer Is there a pharmacy near here?

Suzy Yes, there's one on London Road, next to the coffee shop.

Interviewer Is there a bookstore near here?

Brittany Yeah, it's next to the bank.

1A present tense verb *be*: *I* and *you* + and ?

1.5 Listen and repeat the examples. Then read the rules.

+	
I'm Rob.	(*I'm = I am*)
You're in room 2.	(*You're = You are*)

- *I'm Rob.* NOT ~~Am Rob.~~
- *I'm Rob.* NOT ~~i'm Rob.~~

?		✔	✗	
Am I late?		Yes, **you are**.	No, **you aren't**.	(*aren't = are not*)
Are you Linda?		Yes, **I am**.	No, **I'm not**.	

+	**I'm** late.
?	**Am I** late?

1B present tense verb *be*: *he, she, it* + and ?

1.17 Listen and repeat the examples. Then read the rule.

+	
He's from Brazil.	(*He's = He is*)
She's from Spain.	(*She's = She is*)
It's from China.	(*It's = It is*)

- *he* = man (♂), *she* = woman (♀), *it* = thing

?		✔	✗	
Is he late?		Yes, **he is**.	No, **he isn't**.	(*isn't = is not*)
Is she from Peru?		Yes, **she is**.	No, **she isn't**.	
Is it good?		Yes, **it is**.	No, **it isn't**.	

+	**He's** late.
?	**Is he** late?

? with *What* and *Where*

What's your name?
Where are you from?
Where's he from?

1C present tense verb *be*: *we, you, they*; negatives (all persons)

1.28 Listen and repeat the examples. Then read the rules.

be plural +

We're American.	(*We're = We are*)
You're Japanese.	(*You're = You are*)
They're Peruvian.	(*They're = They are*)

- *we* and *you* = ♂ and ♀
- *you* singular and *you* plural are the same.
- *they* = ♂, ♀, and things

be plural ? and short answers

?	✔	✗	
Are we late?	Yes, **you are**.	No, **you aren't**.	(*aren't = are not*)
Are you from Russia?	Yes, **we are**.	No, **we aren't**.	
Are they Mexican?	Yes, **they are**.	No, **they aren't**.	

be − all persons

+	−
I'm Korean.	**I'm not** Korean.
You're late.	**You aren't** late.
He's Brazilian.	**He isn't** Brazilian.
She's from Mexico.	**She isn't** from Mexico.
It's good.	**It isn't** good.
We're on vacation.	**We aren't** on vacation.
You're in room 10.	**You aren't** in room 10.
They're from Lima.	**They aren't** from Lima.

1A

a Complete with *I'm* or *You're*.

1 **A** Hello. ___*I'm*___ Alex. What's your name?
   B Hi. _____ Anna.

2 **A** _____ in room 1.
   B OK. Thank you.

3 Hello. _____ your teacher.

4 **A** _____ late!
   B Sorry!

b Fill in the blanks. Use contractions where possible.

1 **A** Hello. ___*Are*___ you Ella?
   B No, I'm not. I _____ Lily.

2 **A** _____ I in room 2?
   B No, you _____. You're in room 1.

3 **A** _____ you in class 1?
   B No, I'm _____. I'm in class 2.

4 **A** _____ you Ben?
   B Yes, I _____. Nice to meet you!

5 **A** _____ I late?
   B Yes, you _____!

1B

a Complete with *He's*, *She's*, or *It's*.

   A Where's Istanbul?   **B** ___*It's*___ in Turkey.

1 **A** Where's Siberia?   **B** _____ in Russia.
2 **A** Where's Carolina from? **B** _____ from Brazil.
3 **A** Where's Pedro from?   **B** _____ from Peru.
4 **A** Where's Tokyo?   **B** _____ in Japan.
5 **A** Where's Charles from?   **B** _____ from England.
6 **A** Where's Sofia from?   **B** _____ from Italy.
7 **A** Where's Seattle?   **B** _____ in the United States.
8 **A** Where's Maria from?   **B** _____ from Mexico.

b Complete with *is*, *'s*, or *isn't*.

1 **A** ___*Is*___ Antonio from Mexico?
   B No, he _____. He _____ from Italy.

2 **A** Where _____ Seoul? _____ it in Korea?
   B Yes, it _____.

3 **A** _____ Susan from Chicago?
   B No, she _____ from Miami.

4 **A** Where _____ Boris from?
   B He _____ from Moscow.

5 **A** _____ Scarlett Johansson from England?
   B No, she _____. She _____ from the United States.

1C

a Change the **bold** word(s) to a pronoun, e.g., *you*, *he*, etc.

   Ana and Rafael are from Rio.   ___*They*___ 're from Rio.

1 **Diana and I** are in room 4.   _____ 're in room 4.
2 **The Taj Majal** is in India.   _____ 's in India.
3 Are **Mark and James** in Italy?   Are _____ in Italy?
4 Where is **Rosa** from?   Where's _____ from?
5 **Mira and Rita** are Brazilian.   _____ 're Brazilian.
6 **Paul** isn't in the hotel.   _____ isn't in the hotel.
7 **You and Sara** are in room 2.   _____ 're in room 2.
8 **Jim and I** are from Canada.   _____ 're from Canada.

b Fill in the blanks. Use contractions where possible.

   They ___*aren't*___ Chinese. They ___*'re*___ Japanese, from Tokyo.

1 **A** _____ you from the United States?
   B No, we _____ American. We _____ English.

2 **A** _____ they Spanish?
   B Yes, they _____. They _____ from Madrid.

3 Nikolai _____ from Moscow. He's from St. Petersburg.

4 Sorry, you _____ in room 20. You're in room 22.

5 **A** _____ your name Marco?
   B No, it _____ Marco. It _____ Marcos.

6 **A** _____ we late? **B** Yes, you _____. It _____ 9:30!

7 I _____ Sara Smith. I'm Sara Simpson.

8 They _____ from New York. They're from Texas.

2A singular and plural nouns; *a / an, the*

2.3 Listen and repeat the examples. Then read the rules.

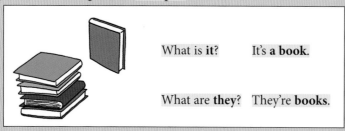

What is **it**?   It's **a book**.

What are **they**?   They're **books**.

Singular	Plural	
1 a book	books	+ *s*
an umbrella	umbrellas	
a day	days	
2 a wat**ch**	wat**ches** /ɪz/	+ *es* (words ending in *ch, sh, s, ss, x*)
3 a dictiona**ry**	dictiona**ries**	*y* + *ies* (words ending in consonant + *y*)

a / an or *the*?

> ***a / an***
> What is it? It's **a** bag. It's **an** umbrella.
> ***the***
> Look at **the** board.
> Open **the** door.
> Close **the** windows.

- Use *a / an* with singular nouns, e.g., ***a*** *book,* **an** *umbrella.*
  Use *an* with words beginning with a vowel (*a, e, i, o, u*), e.g., *an **e**-mail.*
- Don't use *a / an* + plural nouns, e.g., *they're books* NOT ~~they're a books~~.
- Use *the* + singular or plural nouns, e.g., *the door, the windows.*

2B possessive adjectives; possessive *s*

2.9 Listen and repeat the examples. Then read the rules.

Possessive adjectives

I'm from Spain.	**My** name is Ana.
You're American.	**Your** name is Ben.
He's from Rome.	**His** name is Marco.
She's Japanese.	**Her** name is Maki.
It's a parrot.	**Its** name is Polly.
We're from Brazil.	**Our** names are Selma and Luis.
You're Chinese.	**Your** names are Hao-ming and Yi-jun.
They're from Mexico.	**Their** names are Pedro and Maria.

- *your names, our books* NOT ~~yours names, ours books~~
- *its* = for things or animals, e.g., *The Ferrari is a very fast car.* **Its** *top speed is 205 mph.*

2.16 Listen and repeat the examples. Then read the rules.

Possessive *s*

> Miranda is Carrie**'s** friend.
> This is Jack**'s** car.
> Ella is Ben**'s** wife.
> My sister**'s** name is Molly.

- Use *'s* after a person to talk about family and things, e.g., *Ann's brother, Jim's car.*

> ⚠ Ella is Ben**'s** wife. (*'s* = possessive *s*)
> She**'s** American. Her name**'s** Ella. (*'s* = *is*)

2C adjectives

2.23 Listen and repeat the examples. Then read the rules.

> A Ferrari is **expensive**.
> It's a very **fast** car.
> My glasses are **new**.
> They're **old** books.

> ⚠ Use *very* before adjectives, e.g.,
> *It's a very fast car.* NOT ~~It's a fast car very.~~

- Use adjectives:
  – after the verb *be,* e.g., *A Ferrari is expensive.* NOT ~~A Ferrari expensive is.~~
  – before a noun, e.g., *It's a very fast car.* NOT ~~It's a car very fast.~~
- Adjectives are the same for singular and plural:
  It's an old book. They're old books. NOT ~~They're olds books.~~
- Adjectives are the same for ♀ and ♂, e.g., *She's a good girl. He's a good boy.*

2A

a Complete the chart.

Singular	Plural
1 It's a pen.	They're pens.
2 _____.	They're photos.
3 It's a watch.	_____.
4 _____.	They're chairs.
5 It's a dictionary.	_____.
6 It's a credit card.	_____.
7 It's a city.	_____.
8 _____.	They're e-mails.
9 It's a bus.	_____.
10 _____.	They're ID cards.

b Write questions and answers.

What is it?
It's an umbrella.

1 _____ ?
_____

2 _____ ?
_____

3 _____ ?
_____

2B

a Complete with *my, your, his, her, its, your, our,* or *their*.

I'm American. *My* name is William.

1 They're from Japan. _____ names are Ami and Ken.
2 **A** What's _____ name?
   B I'm David. Nice to meet you.
3 He's Peruvian. _____ name is Luis.
4 We're Mexican. _____ names are Antonio and Thalia.
5 That's their cat. _____ name is Felix.
6 _____ name is Tina. She's Brazilian.
7 **A** We're Jane and Mark Kelly.
   B Room 22. This is _____ key.
8 I'm Sally, and this is _____ dog, Rover.

b Write the sentences with the names / people.

This is **his** house. (**my father**) *This is my father's house.*

1 Tom is **her** brother. (**Angela**) _____
2 This is **his** book. (**Antonio**) _____
3 Ann is **his** mother. (**Mark**) _____
4 They're **her** children. (**Yu-ting**) _____
5 **His** car is a Honda. (**my brother**) _____
6 Jim is **her** boyfriend. (**Sally**) _____
7 This is **his** pen. (**Hiro**) _____
8 They're **her** keys. (**my sister**) _____

c Cover sentences 1–8 and look at the sentences on the right (*This is my father's house,* etc.). Say sentences 1–8, e.g., *This is his house.*

2C

a Write sentences with *It's* or *They're*.

1 (great) *It's a great hotel.*

2 (expensive) _____

3 (orange) _____

4 (slow) _____

5 (new) _____

6 (good) _____

b Order the words to make sentences.

blue is bag her
Her bag is blue.

1 fast a car it's.
2 dogs big they're very.
3 photo it's terrible a.
4 a Maria beautiful is very girl.
5 hotel this good a very isn't.
6 very their is small house.
7 new Mark's is laptop.
8 expensive Italian bags are very.

3A   simple present: *I* and *you* +, −, and ?

(3.3) **Listen and repeat the examples. Then read the rules.**

+

> **I live** downtown.
> **You live** near here.

−

> **I don't live** downtown.   (*don't = do not*)
> **You don't live** near here.

- Simple present + is the same for *I* and *you*.
- Simple present − for *I* / *you* = *don't* + verb,
  e.g., *I don't live downtown*. NOT ~~I not live downtown.~~

?   ✔   ✘

> **Do you live** near here?   Yes, **I do.**   No, **I don't.**

- Simple present ? = *Do* + *I* / *you* + verb,
  e.g., ***Do** you live near here?* NOT ~~Live you near here?~~
  Do you live here? Yes, I do. NOT ~~Yes, I live.~~

⚠ **Imperatives**

+ imperative = *Wait! Stand up. Listen*, etc.
− imperative = *Don't* + verb, e.g., *Don't worry.*
              Don't be late, etc.

3B   simple present: *we, you, they* +, −, and ?

(3.10) **Listen and repeat the examples. Then read the rule.**

+

> **We have** coffee for breakfast.
> **You have** rice for lunch.
> **They have** fish for dinner.

−

> **We don't have** tea for breakfast.
> **You don't have** pasta for lunch.
> **They don't have** meat for dinner.

?   ✔   ✘

> **Do you have** eggs for lunch?   Yes, **we do.**   No, **we don't.**
> **Do they have** rice for dinner?   Yes, **they do.**   No, **they don't.**

- Simple present +, −, and ? is the same for *I*, *you*,
  we, *you* (plural), and *they*.

3C   simple present: *he, she, it* +, −, and ?

(3.17) **Listen and repeat the examples. Then read the rules.**

+	**−**	**?**	**✔**	**✘**
I work.	I don't work.	Do I work?	Yes, I do.	No, I don't.
You work.	You don't work.	Do you work?	Yes, you do.	No, you don't.
He works.	**He doesn't work.**	**Does he work?**	**Yes, he does.**	**No, he doesn't.**
She works.	**She doesn't work.**	**Does she work?**	**Yes, she does.**	**No, she doesn't.** (*doesn't = does not*)
It works.	**It doesn't work.**	**Does it work?**	**Yes, it does.**	**No, it doesn't.**
We work.	We don't work.	Do we work?	Yes, we do.	No, we don't.
You work.	You don't work.	Do you work?	Yes, you do.	No, you don't.
They work.	They don't work.	Do they work?	Yes, they do.	No, they don't.

- Simple present *he* / *she* / *it* + = verb + *s*
- Simple present *he* / *she* / *it* − = *doesn't* + verb
- Simple present *he* / *she* / *it* ? = *Does* + *he* / *she* / *it* + verb

Spelling rules 3rd person *s*

I work in an office.	He work**s** in an office. + *s*
I live in Mexico.	He live**s** in Mexico.
I watch CNN.	She watch**es** CNN. + *es*
	(words ending in *ch, sh, ss, x*)
I finish work at 8:00.	The movie finish**es** at 8:00.
I study history.	He stud**ies** history. *y* + *ies*
	(words ending in consonant + *y*)

⚠ **Irregular**   *I have*   *he* / *she* / *it* **has** /hæz/
                  I do   *he* / *she* / *it* **does** /dʌz/
                  I go   *he* / *she* / *it* **goes** /goʊs/

- Spelling rules for 3rd person *s* are the same as for plurals.

3A

a Complete with *do* or *don't*.

I _don't_ live here. I live downtown.

1 **A** _____ you have children?   **B** No, I _____.
2 I _____ like this photo. It's terrible.
3 **A** _____ you want a soda?
  B No, thanks. I _____ drink soda.
4 I _____ have brothers and sisters. I'm an only child.
5 **A** Excuse me, _____ you work here?
  B No, I _____. Sorry.
6 **A** Do you like my coat?   **B** Yes, I _____. It's beautiful.

b Order the words to make sentences or questions.

umbrella have do you an?   *Do you have an umbrella?*

1 like I soccer don't.   _____
2 magazine want you a do?   _____
3 a house I small live in.   _____
4 English you do study?   _____
5 sisters two have I.   _____
6 don't big want a I car.   _____
7 here you near do live?   _____
8 a don't I phone cell have.   _____

3B

a Write sentences.

have tea for breakfast (**They** +)   *They have tea for breakfast.*

1 want coffee or tea (**you** ?)   _____
2 have cereal for breakfast (**They** −)   _____
3 like chocolate (**you** ?)   _____
4 eat a lot of rice in Japan (**We** +)   _____
5 drink coffee in the evening (**you** ?)   _____
6 like Mexican food (**We** −)   _____
7 have salad for lunch (**They** +)   _____
8 drink tea in Russia (**they** ?)   _____

b Complete the sentences with a verb from the list.

drink   have   like   not listen   ~~live~~
read   not speak   watch   work

We _live_ in a big house in Miami.

1 We _____ to the radio in the morning.
2 My husband and I _____ cereal and coffee for breakfast.
3 _____ your children _____ TV at dinner time?
4 My sisters _____ Spanish or Italian.
5 People in Italy _____ a lot of coffee.
6 _____ you _____ on Saturdays?
7 They _____ New York. They think it's a great city.
8 _____ you _____ newspapers and magazines in English?

3C

a Rewrite the sentences.

I live in an apartment.   She _lives in an apartment_____.

1 They read magazines.   He _____.
2 I teach children English. My sister _____.
3 Do you speak English?   _____ he _____?
4 I don't eat fish.   My brother _____.
5 Do you like cats?   _____ she _____?
6 I have two brothers.   Andrew _____.
7 We don't watch TV.   My mother _____.
8 I study French at school. Simon _____.

b Put the verb in (parentheses) in the right form.

They _don't live_ near here. (not live)

1 She _____ to KFMY on the radio. (listen)
2 _____ you _____ meat? (eat)
3 Where _____ she _____? (live)
4 My husband _____ big cars. (not like)
5 What _____ they _____ for breakfast? (have)
6 He _____ TV on the weekend. (watch)
7 _____ he _____ tea or coffee? (want)
8 Carlos _____ soda. (not drink)

4A   simple present + adverbs of frequency: *always, usually, sometimes, never*

4.6 Listen and repeat the examples. Then read the rules.

> I **always** have breakfast.
> They **usually** finish work at 5:00.
> She **sometimes** watches TV in the evening.
> He **never** eats meat.

- Be careful with the <u>position</u> of adverbs of frequency:
  I always have breakfast. NOT ~~Always I have breakfast. I have always breakfast.~~
- With *never*, use a ⊞ verb: *He never eats meat.* NOT ~~He doesn't never eat meat.~~

4B   word order in questions

4.8 Listen and repeat the questions. Then read the rules.

Questions with *be*

Question	Verb	Subject	
	Are	they	American?
	Is	this	your coat?
How old	are	you?	
Where	are	you	from?
What time	is	it?	

- Word order = ⊞ Subject verb **They're** American.
             ? Verb subject **Are they** American?

Questions with *speak, live,* etc.

Question	Auxiliary	Subject	Base form of verb
	Do	you	speak English?
Where	do	you	live?
What	does	your sister	do?
What music	do	you	like?
When	does	Jane	go to the gym?
How	do	you	spell it?

- Word order = Auxiliary, subject, base form
  Do you speak English?
  Question word, auxiliary, subject, base form
  Where do you live?

4C   *can / can't* ⊞, ⊟, and ?

4.13 Listen and repeat the examples. Then read the rules.

can / can't: permission and possibility

⊞

> **You can** park here.
> **He can** come to dinner tonight.
> **We can** have lunch outside.

⊟

> **You can't** park here. (*can't = cannot*)
> **He can't** come to dinner tonight.
> **We can't** have lunch outside.

?   ✔   ✘

> **Can I** park here?   Yes, **you can.**   No, **you can't.**
> **Can they** come to dinner?   Yes, **they can.**   No, **they can't.**

- Use *can / can't* for permission or possibility.
  – *You can park here.* Ⓟ = You have permission.
    You can't park here. = You don't have permission.
  – *I can come to dinner tonight.* = It's possible.
    I can't come to dinner tonight. = It isn't possible.
- *can / can't* is the same for *I, you, he, she,* etc.
- ? = *Can I park here?* NOT ~~Do I can park here?~~

> ⚠ You   1   What do **you** do? I'm a doctor. (singular)
>   2   Where do **you** live? We live in Boston. (plural)
>   3   **You** can't swim here. (= people in general)

4A

a Order the words to make sentences.

drink never coffee after dinner I.
I never drink coffee after dinner.

1 bed I never before to 12:00 go.
2 husband dinner my sometimes makes.
3 a shower take morning the always I in.
4 usually he breakfast has home at.
5 always bus go to they by work.
6 sometimes sandwiches we lunch for have.
7 closes the restaurant late usually.
8 goes work she never shopping after.

b Complete the sentences in the simple present. Use a verb from the list and the **bold** adverb.

do drink ~~eat~~ finish get go have speak watch

He *never eats* meat for lunch. **never**

1 Alex _____ _____ to the gym in the evening. **sometimes**
2 We _____ _____ housework on the weekend. **always**
3 Spanish people _____ _____ lunch at home. **usually**
4 I _____ _____ coffee in the evening. **never**
5 My sister _____ _____ up early. **always**
6 I _____ _____ English at work. **never**
7 We _____ _____ TV after dinner. **sometimes**
8 My husband _____ _____ work at 7:30 p.m. **usually**

4B

a Order the words to make questions.

live you do where? *Where do you live?*

1 show the when TV is?
2 is how mother your?
3 we late are for class?
4 your is this coat?
5 where live Kate does?
6 English does speak brother your?
7 sister sushi does your like?
8 movie start what does time the?

b Complete the sentences with a question word from the list.

How (x2) What (x2) ~~What time~~ When (x2) Where Who

A *What time* do you go to bed? **B** At about eleven o'clock.
1 **A** _____ do you have English classes? **B** On Thursdays.
2 **A** _____ do you want for breakfast? **B** Cereal, please.
3 **A** _____ old is your mother? **B** She's 64.
4 **A** _____ music does she like? **B** Classical music and opera.
5 **A** _____'s that man in the photo? **B** It's my wife's father.
6 **A** _____ do you usually go on vacation? **B** In the summer.
7 **A** _____ does your sister work? **B** In an office.
8 **A** _____ do you spell your last name? **B** I-V-E-R-S-E-N.

4C

a Write sentences with *can* or *can't*.

You / play soccer here −
You can't play soccer here.

1 / we watch TV after dinner ?
2 I / see the board −
3 James / help us tomorrow +
4 / you come to class tomorrow ?
5 You / read my newspaper +
6 We / park here −
7 / I sit here ?
8 She / go to the movies tomorrow −

b Complete the sentences with *can* or *can't* and a verb from the list.

have hear open read remember speak swim walk ~~use~~

You *can use* the Internet in that cafe.

1 **A** _____ we _____ today?
  B No, the water's very cold.
2 I _____ _____ this. I don't have my glasses.
3 **A** What's her sister's name?
  B Sorry, I _____ _____.
4 It's a beautiful day. We _____ _____ lunch outside.
5 **A** Hello, _____ I _____ to John, please?
  B Sorry, he's in a meeting.
6 The restaurant's near here. We _____ _____ there.
7 Sorry, I _____ _____ you very well. Can you say that again?
8 _____ I _____ the window? It's very hot in here.

5

5A simple past: *be*

5.2 Listen and repeat the examples. Then read the rules.

+

I was a teacher.
You were at school yesterday.
He was at home last night.
It was hot last week.
We were at work.
You were in a hurry.
They were in Canada.

−

I wasn't a teacher.	(*wasn't = was not*)
You weren't at school yesterday.	(*weren't = were not*)
He wasn't at home last night.	
It wasn't hot last week.	
We weren't at work.	
You weren't in a hurry.	
They weren't in Canada.	

?   ✔   ✘

	✔	✘
Were you late?	Yes, **I was.**	No, **I wasn't.**
Was she a singer?	Yes, **she was.**	No, **she wasn't.**
Were they in Mexico last week?	Yes, **they were.**	No, **they weren't.**

- Present to past:
  am / is –> **was**, *are* –> **were**
  He **is** at home today.
  He **was** at home yesterday.
- Use *was / were* to talk about the past.
- You can use the simple past with these past time expressions: *this morning, yesterday, last night, last week, last month, last year.*

5B simple past: *have, go, get*

5.11 Listen and repeat the examples. Then read the rules.

+

I got up early yesterday.
You had breakfast in bed.
He went to work by bus.
We got up late today.
You went to school.
They had dinner at home.

−

I didn't get up early yesterday.	(*didn't = did not*)
You didn't have breakfast in bed.	
He didn't go to work by bus.	
We didn't get up late today.	
You didn't go to school.	
They didn't have dinner at home.	

?   ✔   ✘

	✔	✘
Did you go to school yesterday?	Yes, **I did.**	No, **I didn't.**
Did she get up early?	Yes, **she did.**	No, **she didn't.**
Did they have lunch at work?	Yes, **they did.**	No, **they didn't.**

- Use the simple past for finished actions.
- *have, go,* and *get* are **irregular** verbs.
- Present to past:
  + *I have* –> **I had**
  I go –> **I went**
  I get –> **I got**
  − *I don't have / go / get*
  –> **I didn't have / go / get**
  NOT I didn't went
  ? *Do you have / go / get…?*
  –> **Did you have / go / get…?**
  NOT Did you went?
- *Did* is the past of *do.*
- The simple past is the same for all persons.

5C simple past: regular verbs

5.15 Listen and repeat the examples. Then read the rules.

+

I arrived early.
You finished the book.
He wanted a coffee.
The movie ended at 7:00.
We studied Spanish at school.
You worked late.
They stopped at a cafe.

−

I didn't arrive early.
You didn't finish the book.
He didn't want a coffee.
The movie didn't end at 7:00.
We didn't study Spanish at school.
You didn't work late.
They didn't stop at a cafe.

?   ✔   ✘

	✔	✘
Did you watch TV yesterday?	Yes, **I did.**	No, **I didn't.**
Did she walk to work?	Yes, **she did.**	No, **she didn't.**
Did they play tennis?	Yes, **they did.**	No, **they didn't.**

- **regular** past verbs:
  + = verb + *ed*, e.g., *work* –> *work**ed***
- verbs with final *e* = + *d*, e.g., *change* –> *chang**ed***
  verbs with final consonant + *y* = *y* + *ied*, e.g., *cry* –> *cri**ed***
  verbs with final consonant / vowel / consonant = double final consonant + *ed*, e.g., *stop* –> *stop**ped***, *prefer* –> *prefer**red***
- **−** = *I didn't arrive early* NOT I didn't arrived
  ? = *Did you watch TV…?* NOT Did you watched

5A

a Write sentences with *was* and *were*.

We / at home last night [−]   *We weren't at home last night.*

1 / you at school yesterday [?] _____
2 Julia / in the meeting [−] _____
3 We / on a plane at 4:00 [+] _____
4 / they in class yesterday [?] _____
5 David / very happy last night [−] _____
6 I / at work until 8:00 today [+] _____
7 / your sister in Rio last week [?] _____
8 It / a terrible movie [+] _____

b Complete the dialogues with *was*, *wasn't*, *were*, or *weren't*.

A Where [1] *were* you last night?
B I [2] _____ at work all evening.
A No, you [3] _____. You [4] _____ at the movies!
B No, I [5] _____!

A [6] _____ Gloria Estefan a teacher?
B No, she [7] _____. She [8] _____ a translator.

A [9] _____ you in Orlando yesterday?
B No, we [10] _____. We [11] _____ in Miami.

A [12] _____ the movie good?
B No, it [13] _____. It [14] _____ very slow!

5B

a Write the sentences in the simple past with *yesterday*.

I don't go to the gym.
I didn't go to the gym yesterday.

1 She has cereal for breakfast.
2 Do you go to the movies?
3 We don't have lunch.
4 They go home at 8:00.
5 What time do you get up?
6 She doesn't go to school by bus.
7 Jack gets up late.
8 What do you have for dinner?

b Complete the sentences with the **bold** verb in the simple past [+], [−], or [?].

A *Did* you *go* to bed early last night? (**go**)
B Yes, I did. I *went* to bed at 9:30!

1 A What _____ you _____ for lunch today? (**have**)
  B I _____ fish. What's for dinner?
2 Carla _____ to her English class today. (**not go**)
3 A Where _____ you _____ last night? (**go**)
  B We _____ to the theater.
4 A What time _____ the children _____? (**get up**)
  B Late! They _____ at 11:00.
5 I'm very hungry. I _____ breakfast this morning. (**not have**)

5C

a Write the sentences in the simple past.

He studies a lot.
He studied a lot.

1 We work in a bank.
2 He finishes work late.
3 They live in Brazil.
4 I worry a lot.
5 She walks to work.
6 The train stops in Kyoto.
7 We play tennis.
8 You talk a lot!

b Complete the dialogues with the **bold** verb in the simple past [+], [−], or [?].

A *Did* you *play* golf last weekend? (**play**)
B Yes, I *played* on Saturday.

1 A Where _____ you _____ the car? (**park**)
  B I _____ it near the restaurant.
2 A _____ you _____ your homework? (**finish**)
  B No, I _____ it. It was very late.
3 A What _____ you _____ in college? (**study**)
  B I _____ economics.
4 A _____ you _____ the movie? (**like**)
  B No, I _____ it very much. The actors were terrible.
5 A _____ you _____ TV last night? (**watch**)
  B Yes, we _____ a very good show.
6 A _____ you _____ the door when you went out? (**close**)
  B Of course I _____ it!

6A   there is / there are

(6.4)   **Listen and repeat the examples. Then read the rules.**

Singular	
+	**There's** a TV. **There's** a bathtub.
−	**There isn't** a phone. **There isn't** a lamp.

Plural	
+	**There are** two beds. **There are** some pictures.
−	**There aren't** any towels. **There aren't** any pillows.

Singular			
?	**Is there** a parking lot?	✔	Yes, **there is.**
?	**Is there** a gym?	✘	No, **there isn't.**

Plural			
?	**Are there** any elevators?	✔	Yes, **there are.**
?	**Are there** any cabinets?	✘	No, **there aren't.**

- *There's a TV in my hotel room.* = the room has a TV
- Use *some* and *any* + plural nouns.
- *some* = you don't say how many.
- *some* changes to *any* for − and ?.
- Don't contract *there is* in short answers, e.g., *Yes, there is.* NOT ~~Yes, there's.~~

6B   there was / there were

(6.9)   **Listen and repeat the examples. Then read the rules.**

Singular	
+	**There was** a train station. **There was** a road.
−	**There wasn't** an airport. **There wasn't** a swimming pool.

Plural	
+	**There were** some hotels. **There were** ten cafes.
−	**There weren't** any big stores. **There weren't** any tall buildings.

Singular			
?	**Was there** a park?	✔	Yes, **there was.**
?	**Was there** a shopping mall?	✘	No, **there wasn't.**

Plural			
?	**Were there** any hotels?	✔	Yes, **there were.**
?	**Were there** any restaurants?	✘	No, **there weren't.**

- *there was / there were* is the past tense of *there is / there are*
- *some / any* (See **6A** *there is / there are*)

6C   object pronouns

(6.18)   **Listen and repeat the examples. Then read the rule.**

Subject pronoun	Object pronoun
I'm your teacher.	Do you want to talk to **me**?
You're lost.	Can I help **you**?
He was at the party.	I saw **him**.
She never listens.	Don't talk to **her**.
It's a beautiful coat!	I want **it** for my birthday.
We aren't friends.	They don't speak to **us**.
They're good books.	Why don't you read **them**?

- Use object pronouns (*me*, *him*, etc.) as the object of a verb or after prepositions.

6A

a Complete with *a*, *some*, or *any*.

Are there _any_ elevators?

1 There aren't _____ cars in the parking lot.
2 There are _____ pillows on the bed.
3 There's _____ sauna in the spa.
4 Are there _____ chairs in the room?
5 Is there _____ TV in the restaurant?
6 There isn't _____ table in the bedroom.
7 There aren't _____ windows in my room.
8 There are _____ stores in the hotel.

b Complete with the right form of *there is* or *there are*.

There aren't any sodas in the kitchen.

1 _____ any free tables in the restaurant?
2 _____ any elevators in the hotel.
3 _____ a bathtub in the bathroom. It's very big.
4 _____ a swimming pool in the hotel?
5 _____ a remote control for the TV.
6 _____ any pictures in the room.
7 _____ a meeting room in the hotel?
8 _____ some towels on the floor.

6B

a Write the sentences in the past.

There's a big parking lot. _There was a big parking lot._

1 Is there an airport? _____
2 There aren't any restaurants. _____
3 There are a lot of stores. _____
4 There aren't any cafes. _____
5 Are there any tourists? _____
6 There isn't a spa. _____
7 Is there a bank? _____
8 There's a hospital. _____

b Complete the dialogue with the right form of *there was* or *there were*.

A Hi, Jack. How was the hotel?
B It was awful.
A Why?
B Well, ¹ _there wasn't_ an elevator, and our room was on the third floor. The room was big, but it was cold and dark, and ² _____ any windows.
A ³ _____ a restaurant?
B No, ⁴ _____. ⁵ _____ only a cafe.
A ⁶ _____ a lot of people in the hotel?
B No. And I'm not surprised.
A ⁷ _____ a swimming pool?
B Yes, ⁸ _____, but it wasn't very clean.

6C

a Change the **highlighted** words to <u>one</u> pronoun.

I didn't see Maria in class yesterday.
I didn't see _her_ in class yesterday.

1 I never talk to Tom.
2 We're lost! Can you help my friend and me?
3 I call my mother and father every weekend.
4 I read this book last year.
5 Can't you find your keys?
6 I don't like Jack Nicholson in that movie.
7 Do you love your wife?
8 Wait for Jane and me!
9 I don't know his phone number.
10 Did you tell Luisa about the meeting?

b Complete the sentences with an object pronoun.

You speak very fast. I can't understand _you_.

1 I bought a camera, but I left _____ in the store.
2 Jim likes Sarah, but she doesn't like _____.
3 My children love stories. I read to _____ every night.
4 Emma said good-bye to Jack, and he kissed _____.
5 I'm hungry. Can you make _____ a sandwich, please?
6 We saw them at the airport, but they didn't see _____.
7 I don't have my car today. Can I go with _____?

7A present continuous: *be* + verb + *-ing*

7.3 Listen and repeat the examples. Then read the rules.

+	**–**
I'm working today.	**I'm not working** today.
You're sitting in my chair.	**You aren't sitting** in my chair.
He's playing soccer.	**He isn't playing** soccer.
It's snowing.	**It isn't snowing.**
We're having dinner.	**We aren't having** dinner.
They're watching TV.	**They aren't watching** TV.

?	**✔**	**✘**
Are you working today?	Yes, **I am.**	No, **I'm not.**
Is she studying?	Yes, **she is.**	No, **she isn't.**
Is it snowing?	Yes, **it is.**	No, **it isn't.**
Are they watching TV?	Yes, **they are.**	No, **they aren't.**

- Use *be* + verb + *-ing* to talk about things that are happening now.
- Spelling rules for the *-ing* form:

Base form	Verb + *-ing*	Spelling
read study	rea**ding** study**ing**	+ *-ing*
drive	dri**ving**	~~e~~ + *-ing*
swim	swi**mming**	one-syllable verbs: one vowel + one consonant = double consonant + *-ing*

7B future: *be going to* (plans)

7.7 Listen and repeat the examples. Then read the rules.

+	**–**
I'm going to come to class on Friday.	**I'm not going to** come to class on Friday.
You're going to go to Paris this weekend.	**You aren't going to** go to Paris this weekend.
He's going to buy a new car.	**He isn't going to** buy a new car.
We're going to camp.	**We aren't going to** camp.
They're going to stay with us.	**They aren't going to** stay with us.

?	**✔**	**✘**
Are you going to travel?	Yes, **I am.**	No, **I'm not.**
Is she going to see them?	Yes, **she is.**	No, **she isn't.**
Are they going to swim?	Yes, **they are.**	No, **they aren't.**

- Use *be* + *going to* + verb to talk about future plans.
- You can use future time expressions, e.g., *tomorrow*, *next week*, etc.

7C future: *be going to* (predictions)

7.13 Listen and repeat the examples. Then read the rule.

1 **It's going to** rain.
2 I think **you're going to** like it.
3 What's **going to** happen next?
4 **They're going to** have a great time in New York.

- You can use *be* + *going to* + verb to make predictions for the future.

7A

a Write sentences in the present continuous.

He / take a shower   *He's taking a shower.*

1 I / work _____
2 She / play tennis _____
3 They / swim _____
4 He / make dinner _____
5 I / study _____
6 She / read _____
7 They / have breakfast _____
8 He / park the car _____

b Complete the sentences with the **bold** verb in the present continuous ⊞, ⊟ or ⍰.

She *is eating* pasta. (**eat**)

1 Look! It _____ . (**snow**)
2 **A** Excuse me! You _____ in my seat. **B** Sorry! (**sit**)
3 **A** What _____ you _____ here? **B** I _____ for a friend (**do, wait**)
4 I can go shopping with you. I _____ today! (**not work**)
5 **A** _____ Alice _____ her homework? (**do**)
   B No, she isn't. She _____ to her boyfriend. (**talk**)
6 **A** Where _____ you _____? **B** To the beach! (**go**)
7 **A** Where _____ your brother _____ in New York? **B** At a hotel. (**stay**)

7B

a Write sentences with the right form of *be going to.*

/ he / come tonight ⍰
 Is he going to come tonight?

1 They / take the train to Chicago ⊞
2 She / go to college ⊟
3 We / get married next summer ⊞
4 / you / go out for dinner ⍰
5 / he / pay you the money ⍰
6 I / study this evening ⊟
7 / you / meet us at the airport ⍰
8 She / make pasta for lunch ⊞

b Complete with *(be) going to* and a verb from the list.

| buy do ~~give~~ go not have meet send not stay wear |

I *'m going to give* _____ her a book for her birthday.

1 We _____ a new car next month.
2 _____ you _____ him an e-mail?
3 **A** What _____ you _____ tonight?   **B** I'm going to see a movie.
4 They _____ a vacation this year.
5 We _____ in that hotel. It's very expensive!
6 I'm tired. I _____ to bed early this evening.
7 It's cold outside. _____ you _____ a coat?
8 He _____ us outside the theater at 7:00.

7C

What's going to happen? Write a sentence for each picture.

1 be very hot
 They're going to
 be very hot!

2 make a pizza
_____
_____

3 leave soon
_____
_____

4 tell them a story
_____
_____

5 rain tomorrow
_____
_____
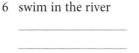

6 swim in the river
_____
_____

7 break his leg
_____
_____

8 be late for school
_____
_____

Numbers

A Numbers 0–10

a 🔊 **1.7** Listen 👂 and repeat the numbers.

0 zero
1 one /wʌn/
2 two /tu/
3 three
4 four
5 five
6 six
7 seven
8 eight /eɪt/
9 nine
10 ten

> 0 = oh /oʊ/ in room numbers, e.g., room 207 (two oh seven).

b Cover ✋ the words. Say the numbers.

◀ p.5

B Numbers 11–20

a 🔊 **1.34** Listen and repeat the numbers.

11 eleven
12 twelve
13 thirteen /θər'tin/
14 fourteen
15 fifteen
16 sixteen
17 seventeen
18 eighteen
19 nineteen
20 twenty

b Cover ✋ the words. Say the numbers.

◀ p.9

C Numbers 21–100

a 🔊 **2.31** Listen and repeat the numbers.

21 twenty-one
22 twenty-two
30 thirty
33 thirty-three
40 forty
44 forty-four
50 fifty
55 fifty-five
60 sixty
66 sixty-six
70 seventy
77 seventy-seven
80 eighty
88 eighty-eight
90 ninety
99 ninety-nine
100 a/one hundred

> ⚠ 30 thirty   13 thirteen
> 40 forty   14 fourteen etc.

b Cover ✋ the words. Say the numbers.

◀ p.20

Study Link MultiROM www.oup.com/elt/americanenglishfile/starter

A Countries

a **1.13** Listen and repeat the countries.

 Brazil

 China

 England /ˈɪŋɡlənd/

 Italy

 Japan

 Korea

 Mexico

 Peru

 Russia /ˈrʌʃə/

 Spain

 Turkey /ˈtərki/

 the United States

---

the US = the United States
the UK = the United Kingdom
Country names begin with a CAPITAL letter,
e.g., Brazil NOT ~~brazil~~.

---

b Cover the words. Look at the pictures. Say the countries.

c Write your country: _____.
Practice saying it.

⊙ p.6

B Nationalities

a **1.24** Listen and repeat the countries and nationalities.

Country	Nationality
Brazil	Brazilian
China	Chinese
England	English
Italy	Italian
Japan	Japanese
Korea	Korean
Mexico	Mexican
Peru	Peruvian
Russia	Russian
Spain	Spanish
Turkey	Turkish
the United States	American
the UK	British

b Cover the words. Look at the flags. Say the country and nationality.

Brazil — Brazilian

c Write your nationality: _____.
Practice saying it.

⚠ *English*, *Spanish*, etc. = nationality and language. They begin with a CAPITAL letter, e.g., English NOT ~~english~~.

---

d Complete the sentences about you.

I'm _____, and I'm _____. (name, nationality)
I'm from _____ in _____. (town / city, country)

⊙ p.8

Things

A Things in the classroom

a **1.47** Listen and repeat the words.

1 the board /bɔrd/
2 the door /dɔr/
3 a <u>win</u>dow /ˈwɪndoʊ/
4 a <u>ta</u>ble
5 a chair
6 a coat /koʊt/
7 a <u>lap</u>top
8 a book
9 a <u>dic</u>tionary
10 a piece of <u>pa</u>per

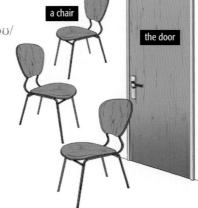

a chair

the door

b Cover 🖐 the words. Look at the picture. Say the things.

↩ p.11

B Small things

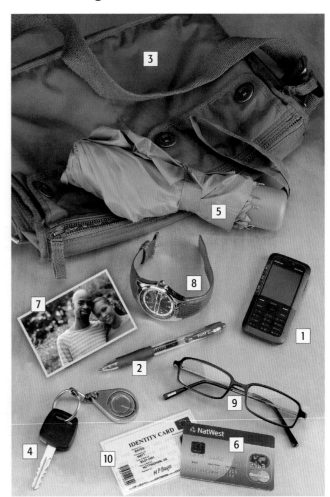

a **2.1** Listen and repeat the words.

1 a cell phone
2 a pen
3 a bag
4 a key /ki/
5 an um<u>brel</u>la
6 a <u>cred</u>it card
7 a <u>pho</u>to
8 a watch
9 <u>glass</u>es /ˈɡlæsəz/
10 an <u>ID</u> card

> ⚠ **a** key, **a** bag BUT **an** umbrella, **an** ID card

b Cover 🖐 the words. Look at the photo. Say the things.

↩ p.14

Study Link MultiROM www.oup.com/elt/americanenglishfile/starter

People

a 🔊 **2.10** Listen and repeat the words.

1 a boy
2 a girl
3 a man
4 a woman /ˈwʊmən/
5 children
6 friends /frɛndz/

b Cover ✋ the words. Look at the photos. Say the people.

c 🔊 **2.11** Listen and repeat the irregular plurals.

⚠ Irregular plurals	
Singular	**Plural**
a child /tʃaɪld/	children /ˈtʃɪldrən/
a man	men
a woman	women /ˈwɪmən/
a person	people /ˈpipl/

d Cover ✋ the plural words. Say them.

Family

a 🔊 **2.12** Listen and repeat the words.

1 husband
2 wife
3 mother /ˈmʌðər/
4 father /ˈfɑðər/
5 son /sʌn/
6 daughter /ˈdɔtər/
7 sister
8 brother
9 boyfriend
10 girlfriend

b Cover ✋ the words. Look at the photos. Say the people.

c Work with a partner.

A (Book open) How do you spell *friend*?
B (Book closed) F-R-E-N-D.
A No. F-R-I-E-N-D.

⬅ p.16

Adjectives

Colors

a 2.20 Listen and repeat the words.

red 1

green 2

yellow /ˈyɛloʊ/ 3

blue 4

orange /ˈɔrɪndʒ/ 5

brown /braʊn/ 6

black 7

white 8

b Cover 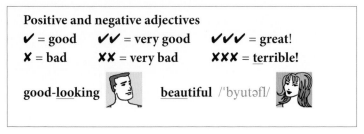 the words. Look at the photos. Say the colors.

Common adjectives

a 2.21 Listen and repeat the words.

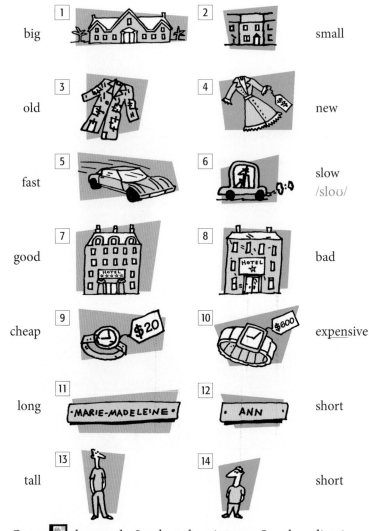

1 big

2 small

3 old

4 new

5 fast

6 slow /sloʊ/

7 good

8 bad

9 cheap

10 expensive

11 long

12 short

13 tall

14 short

b Cover the words. Look at the pictures. Say the adjectives.

c Test a partner.

A What's the opposite of *new*?
B *Old*. What's the opposite of _____?

d 2.22 Listen and repeat the positive and negative adjectives.

> **Positive and negative adjectives**
> ✔ = good   ✔✔ = very good   ✔✔✔ = great!
> ✗ = bad   ✗✗ = very bad   ✗✗✗ = terrible!
>
> good-looking   beautiful /ˈbyutəfl/

p.18

a **3.4** Listen and repeat the phrases.

live in an apartment /lɪv/

have children

watch TV /wɑtʃ/

listen to the radio /'lɪsn/

read magazines

eat fast food

drink coffee

speak English

want a new car /wɑnt/

like dogs

work in a bank /wərk/

study Spanish

b **3.5** Cover the words. Listen and say the phrase.

"in an apartment"

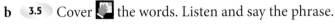 live in an apartment

c Make true ⊕ or ⊖ sentences about you.

1 I watch _____ on TV. (a TV show)
  I don't watch _____.
2 I speak _____. (a language)
  I don't speak _____.
3 I listen to _____. (a radio station)
  I don't listen to _____.
4 I read _____. (a magazine)
  I don't read _____.
5 I drink _____. (a drink)
  I don't drink _____.

● p.24

Food and drink

a **3.9** Listen and repeat the words.

FOOD

1. fish
2. meat
3. pasta
4. rice
5. eggs

6. salad
7. vegetables /ˈvɛdʒtəblz/
8. potatoes
9. fruit /frut/

10. bread /brɛd/
11. a sandwich
12. butter
13. cheese
14. cereal /ˈsɪriəl/
15. sugar /ˈʃʊgər/
16. chocolate /ˈtʃɑklət/

DRINK

17. coffee
18. tea
19. milk
20. water /ˈwɔtər/
21. orange juice /dʒus/
22. soda /ˈsoʊdə/

Meals

breakfast (in the morning)
lunch (in the afternoon)
dinner (in the evening)
What do you have for breakfast? (*have* = eat and / or drink),
e.g., *I have cereal and coffee.*

b Cover the words. Look at the photos. Say the words.

c Practice with a partner.

> Do you like…?
>
> Yes, I do. / No, I don't.

○ p.26

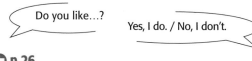 **Study Link** **MultiROM** www.oup.com/elt/americanenglishfile/starter

What do they do?

a **3.20** Listen and repeat the words.

a <u>tea</u>cher   a <u>doc</u>tor   a <u>nurse</u> /nərs/   a <u>sales</u>person   a <u>wai</u>ter (a <u>wai</u>tress)

an a<u>ssist</u>ant   a <u>law</u>yer /ˈlɔyər/   a po<u>lice</u>man (a po<u>lice</u>woman)   a <u>fac</u>tory worker   a <u>stu</u>dent /ˈstudnt/

b Cover the words. Ask and answer in pairs.

> What does she do?

> She's a teacher. What does he do?

c **3.21** Listen and repeat the sentences.

> He works for Microsoft®.
> He's in school.
> She's in college.
> She's at a university.
>   She studies economics.
> He doesn't have a job.
> She's re<u>tired</u>. /rɪˈtaɪərd/

d What do <u>you</u> do?

I _____

.

Where do they work?

a **3.22** Listen and repeat the phrases.

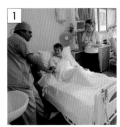

in a <u>hos</u>pital   in a store   in a <u>res</u>taurant   in an <u>of</u>fice

in a school   in a <u>fac</u>tory   **at** home   **on** the street

b Cover the phrases. Look at the photos. Say the phrases.

c Ask and answer with a partner.

> Where does a doctor work?

> In a hospital.

d Where do <u>you</u> work?

I _____

.

◐ p.29

A What time is it?

a `3.27` Listen and repeat the times.

It's one (o'clock).

It's five after one.

It's ten after one.

It's <u>quarter</u> after one.
/ˈkwɔrtər/

It's <u>twenty</u> after one.

It's twenty-five after one.

It's one thirty.

It's twenty-five to two.

It's twenty to two.

It's quarter to two.

It's ten to two.

It's five to two.

b Cover the times. Look at the clocks and say the times.

⟲ p.30

B Ordinal numbers

a `5.20` Listen and repeat the ordinal numbers from 1st–20th.

1st the first	11th the el<u>even</u>th	21st the twenty-<u>first</u>	31st the thirty-<u>first</u>
2nd the <u>second</u>	12th the twelfth	22nd the twenty-<u>second</u>	
3rd the third	13th the thir<u>teen</u>th	23rd the twenty-<u>third</u>	
4th the fourth	14th the four<u>teen</u>th	24th the twenty-<u>fourth</u>	
5th the fifth	15th the fif<u>teen</u>th	25th the twenty-<u>fifth</u>	
6th the sixth	16th the six<u>teen</u>th	26th the twenty-<u>sixth</u>	
7th the <u>seven</u>th	17th the seven<u>teen</u>th	27th the twenty-<u>seven</u>th	
8th the eighth	18th the eigh<u>teen</u>th	28th the twenty-<u>eigh</u>th	
9th the ninth	19th the nine<u>teen</u>th	29th the twenty-<u>ninth</u>	
10th the tenth	20th the <u>twenty</u>ieth	30th the <u>thirty</u>eth	

b Practice saying the ordinal numbers from 21st–31st.

⟲ p.50

a **4.3** Listen and repeat the phrases.

In the <u>morning</u>

get up

have <u>break</u>fast

take a <u>show</u>er

go to work
(by bus, car, etc.)

go to school

have a <u>coffee</u>

have a
<u>sand</u>wich

In the after<u>noon</u>

have lunch

<u>fi</u>nish work

go home

go <u>shop</u>ping

go to the gym
/dʒɪm/

In the <u>eve</u>ning

make <u>din</u>ner

have <u>din</u>ner

do <u>house</u>work

watch T<u>V</u>

go to bed

> ⚠ **make** dinner / coffee BUT **do** housework
> ⚠ go **to the** gym, **to the** movies, etc.
>   go **to** work, **to** school, **to** bed
>   go home

b **4.4** Listen and point to the picture.

c In pairs, look at the pictures and describe their day.

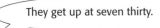

They get up at seven thirty.

They have breakfast.

◐ p.34

Common verbs 2

A

a (4.9) Listen and repeat the verbs and verb phrases.

go to the <u>mo</u>vies

[1]

play computer games

[6]

go to the <u>thea</u>ter
/ˈθɪətər/

[2]

play sports

[7]

go to the beach

[3]

ski

[8]

play <u>ten</u>nis

[4]

walk

[9]

play the <u>pia</u>no

[5]

swim

[10]

b Cover the words. Look at the pictures. Say the verbs or phrases.

c Work in pairs. Make true sentences with *sometimes* or *never*.

> I sometimes go to the movies.

> I never go to the theater.

🡢 p.37

B

a (4.17) Listen and repeat the verbs and verb phrases.

take a break

[1]

change <u>mo</u>ney

[2]

use the <u>In</u>ternet

[3]

take <u>pho</u>tos

[4]

drive

[5]

pay by <u>cre</u>dit card

[6]

park

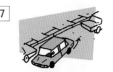

[7]

come

[8]

see

[9]

hear

[10]

b Cover the words. Look at the pictures. Say the verbs or phrases.

🡢 p.39

Study Link MultiROM www.oup.com/elt/americanenglishfile/starter

A

a 5.18 Listen and repeat the verb phrases.

1		arrive at the airport	6	 learn a language
2		break your leg /breɪk/	7	 meet a friend
3		buy a ticket /baɪ/	8	 rent a car
4		come back from vacation	9	 say hello
5		find a job /faɪnd/	10	stay at a hotel

> **arrive** in a country / city, e.g., Italy, Rome
> at a building, e.g., the airport, a friend's house

meet a person for the first time

meet at the train station

meet friends after work

b Cover the verb phrases. Look at the pictures. Say the phrases.

⬅ p.48

B

a 6.13 Listen and repeat the verb phrases.

1	call a friend	6	 send an e-mail
2	get a letter	7	 take an umbrella
3	give a present	8	tell somebody a story
4	leave the house	9	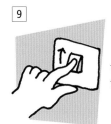 turn on the light
5	lose your keys /luz/	10	 turn off the light

b Cover the verb phrases. Look at the pictures. Say the phrases.

⬅ p.58

Study Link MultiROM www.oup.com/elt/americanenglishfile/starter

Hotels

In a hotel bedroom

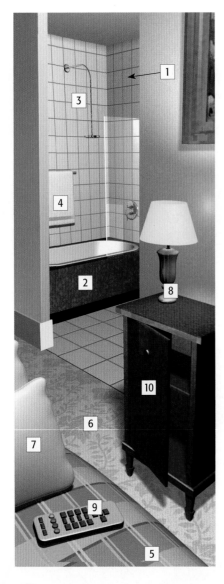

a **6.1** Listen and repeat the words.

1 the <u>bath</u>room
2 a <u>bath</u>tub
3 a <u>show</u>er
4 a <u>tow</u>el /ˈtaʊəl/
5 a bed
6 the floor
7 a <u>pil</u>low /ˈpɪloʊ/
8 a lamp
9 a re<u>mote</u> con<u>trol</u>
10 a <u>cab</u>inet /ˈkæbənət/

b Cover ✋ the words. Look at the picture. Say the words.

In a hotel

a **6.2** Listen and repeat the words.

1 a cafe
2 a <u>park</u>ing lot
3 a yard
4 a <u>gift</u> shop
5 a gym
6 an <u>el</u>evator
7 re<u>cep</u>tion
8 a <u>res</u>taurant
9 a spa /spɑ/
10 a <u>swim</u>ming pool
11 <u>bath</u>rooms

b Cover ✋ the words. Look at the picture. Say the words.

c Practice with a partner. Ask and answer.

> Where's the swimming pool?

> It's on the fifth floor.

⟳ p.54

Places

a **6.7** Listen and repeat the words.

1 a city /ˈsɪti/
2 a town
3 a village

4 an airport
5 a bank
6 a beach
7 a pharmacy /ˈfɑrməsi/
8 a church
9 a movie theater
10 a hospital
11 a museum /myuˈziəm/
12 a park
13 a gas station
14 a post office
15 a river /ˈrɪvər/
16 a road
17 the ocean
18 a store
19 a train station
20 a supermarket

b Cover the words. Look at the pictures. Say the places.

c Do you live in a village, town, or city? Make true sentences about the place where you live:

There's a / an…
There isn't a / an…
There are two / three…
There are some…
There are a lot of…
There aren't any…

> I live in a small town.
> There's a post office.
> There isn't an airport.

○ p.56

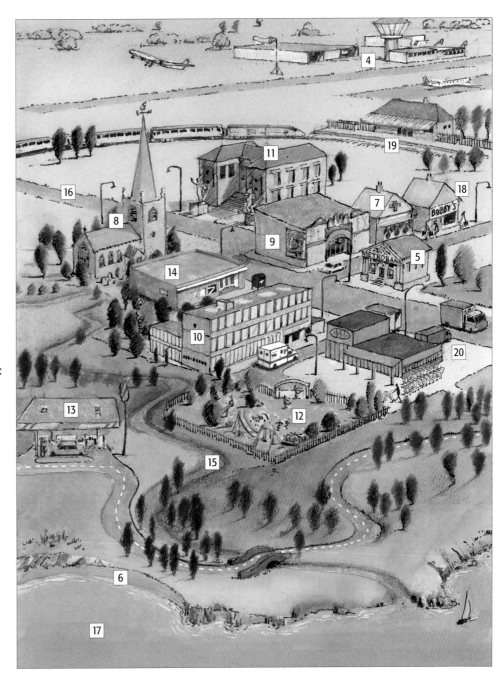

Irregular verbs

a 6.17 Listen and repeat the irregular verbs in the present and the past, e.g., *is – was*.

b Cover 🖐 the **PAST** column. Practice saying the sentences in the past.

PRESENT		PAST
is	It ▨▨▨▨ very hot yesterday.	was
are	They ▨▨▨▨ in Brazil last week.	were
begin	It ▨▨▨▨ to snow.	began
break	I'm sorry I ▨▨▨▨ the window!	broke
buy	We ▨▨▨▨ some food at the market.	bought /bɔt/
can	She ▨▨▨▨ speak Russian when she was four.	could /kəd/
come	They ▨▨▨▨ to class last week.	came
do	I ▨▨▨▨ my homework in the evening.	did
drink	We ▨▨▨▨ a lot of coffee.	drank
drive	He ▨▨▨▨ very fast because he was in a hurry.	drove
eat	I ▨▨▨▨ a lot yesterday.	ate
find	They ▨▨▨▨ an apartment downtown.	found
get	We ▨▨▨▨ up early this morning.	got
give	I ▨▨▨▨ Anna a birthday present.	gave
go	They ▨▨▨▨ on vacation in July.	went
have	I ▨▨▨▨ my old car for 15 years.	had
hear	We ▨▨▨▨ a noise during the night.	heard /hərd/
know	I ▨▨▨▨ all the answers.	knew /nu/
leave	The train ▨▨▨▨ the station at 8:00.	left
lose	I ▨▨▨▨ my keys on the train.	lost
make	John ▨▨▨▨ dinner last night.	made
meet	I ▨▨▨▨ a lot of people at the university.	met
pay	I ▨▨▨▨ by credit card in the restaurant.	paid /peɪd/
read	They ▨▨▨▨ a lot of books on vacation.	read /rɛd/
ride	We ▨▨▨▨ our bikes in the park.	rode /roʊd/
say	I ▨▨▨▨ I was sorry.	said /sɛd/
see	I ▨▨▨▨ an old friend at the party.	saw /sɔ/
send	He ▨▨▨▨ a lot of e-mails.	sent
sit	They ▨▨▨▨ near the window.	sat
sleep	I ▨▨▨▨ for eight hours last night.	slept
speak	We ▨▨▨▨ Chinese to the waiter.	spoke
swim	I ▨▨▨▨ every day when I was in Mexico.	swam
take	Jane ▨▨▨▨ good photos of the house.	took /tʊk/
tell	I ▨▨▨▨ my children a story last night.	told
think	We ▨▨▨▨ the music was terrible.	thought /θɔt/
wear	I ▨▨▨▨ my new boots to the party.	wore
write	She ▨▨▨▨ a lot of e-mails this morning.	wrote

Study Link **MultiROM** www.oup.com/elt/americanenglishfile/starter

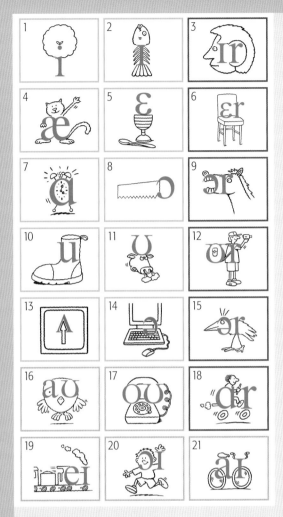

■ voiced
■ unvoiced

■ vowels followed by /r/
■ diphthongs

1 tree /tri/
2 fish /fɪʃ/
3 ear /ɪr/
4 cat /kæt/
5 egg /ɛg/
6 chair /tʃɛr/
7 clock /klɑk/
8 saw /sɔ/
9 horse /hɔrs/
10 boot /but/
11 bull /bʊl/

12 tourist /'tʊrɪst/
13 up /ʌp/
14 computer /kəm'pyutər/
15 bird /bərd/
16 owl /aʊl/
17 phone /foʊn/
18 car /kɑr/
19 train /treɪn/
20 boy /bɔɪ/
21 bike /baɪk/

22 parrot /'pærət/
23 bag /bæg/
24 keys /kiz/
25 girl /gərl/
26 flower /'flaʊər/
27 vase /veɪs/
28 tie /taɪ/
29 dog /dɔg/
30 snake /sneɪk/
31 zebra /'zibrə/
32 shower /'ʃaʊər/
33 television /'tɛləvɪʒn/

34 thumb /θʌm/
35 mother /'mʌðər/
36 chess /tʃɛs/
37 jazz /dʒæz/
38 leg /lɛg/
39 right /raɪt/
40 witch /wɪtʃ/
41 yacht /yɑt/
42 monkey /'mʌŋki/
43 nose /noʊz/
44 singer /'sɪŋər/
45 house /haʊs/

	usual spelling	⚠ but also
tree	**ee** three meet **ea** please read **e** she we	people key piece
fish	**i** Italy six is it big window	English women gym
ear	**eer** cheer **ere** here we're **ear** near year	
cat	**a** bag thanks black man bad that	
egg	**e** spell ten seven twenty Mexico	friend breakfast bread
chair	**air** airport upstairs haircut **are** careful	their there where
clock	**o** not hot stop hospital	what watch want
saw	**al** talk walk **aw** saw draw awful	water bought daughter
horse	**or** short important door	four board
boot	**oo** too food **u*** excuse blue **ew** new	two you juice

	usual spelling	⚠ but also
bull	**u** full sugar **oo** good book look cook	woman could
tourist	A very unusual sound. euro Europe sure plural	
up	**u** umbrella number bus husband but	son brother double
computer	Many different spellings. ə is always unstressed. pocket seven famous about children	
bird	**er** person verb **ir** first third **ur** nurse Turkey	work word world
owl	**ou** out house pound sound **ow** town down	
phone	**o*** open close no hello **oa** coat	window
car	**ar** are park start far	heart
train	**a*** name late **ai** e-mail Spain **ay** day say	eight they great
boy	**oi** coin noise **oy** boyfriend enjoy	
bike	**i*** I Hi nice **y** bye my **igh** night flight	buy

* especially before consonant + **e**

	usual spelling		⚠ but also
parrot	**p**	paper pillow sleep top	
	pp	stopped happen	
bag	**b**	board British remember job	
	bb	rubber	
keys	**c**	come cold	school
	k	ski take	
	ck	back clock	
girl	**g**	go green big blog	
	gg	eggs	
flower	**f**	fifteen Friday wife	
	ph	photo phone	
	ff	office coffee	
vase	**v**	TV very have live seven five	of
tie	**t**	time tell start late	liked finished
	tt	letter butter	
dog	**d**	did drink study good	played cried
	dd	address middle	
snake	**s**	small fast	nice city
	ss	stress waitress	
zebra	**z**	zero Brazil	
	s	bags cars husband easy	
shower	**sh**	shop she Spanish finish	sugar sure
	ti	information	
	(+ vowel)	reservation	
television	An unusual sound. usually usual		

	usual spelling		⚠ but also
thumb	**th**	thing think tenth birthday month Thursday	
mother	**th**	the father weather their brother they	
chess	**ch**	children lunch	
	tch	watch kitchen	
	t (+ure)	picture	
jazz	**j**	Japan juice job	gym page
	dge	bridge	
leg	**l**	lamp listen plan table	
	ll	small umbrella	
right	**r**	red rice problem children	write wrong
	rr	terrible married	
witch	**w**	watch twenty word we	one
	wh	what white where	
yacht	**y**	yellow your yes you	
	before u	music university	
monkey	**m**	mountain Monday September come	
	mm	summer swimming	
nose	**n**	nine never men piano	know
	nn	sunny dinner	
singer	**ng**	thing long doing going playing wrong	think thank
house	**h**	hello hi how hotel have hurry	who

OXFORD
UNIVERSITY PRESS

198 Madison Avenue
New York, NY 10016 USA

Great Clarendon Street, Oxford OX2 6DP UK

Oxford University Press is a department of the University of Oxford. It furthers the University's objective of excellence in research, scholarship, and education by publishing worldwide in

Oxford New York

Auckland Cape Town Dar es Salaam Hong Kong Karachi Kuala Lumpur Madrid Melbourne Mexico City Nairobi New Delhi Shanghai Taipei Toronto

With offices in

Argentina Austria Brazil Chile Czech Republic France Greece Guatemala Hungary Italy Japan Poland Portugal Singapore South Korea Switzerland Thailand Turkey Ukraine Vietnam

OXFORD and OXFORD ENGLISH are registered trademarks of Oxford University Press in certain countries.

© Oxford University Press 2010

Database right Oxford University Press (maker)

Editorial Director: Laura Pearson
Executive Publishing Manager: Erik Gundersen
Development Editor: Hannah Ryu
Design Director: Susan Sanguily
Design Manager: Stacy Merlin
Senior Production Artist: Julie Armstrong
Production Artist: Colleen Ho
Image Editor: Robin Fadool
Design Production Manager: Stephen White
Production Editor: Alissa Heyman
Manufacturing Manager: Shanta Persaud
Manufacturing Coordintor: Faye Wang

ISBN: 978-0-19-477400-0

Printed in China

10 9 8 7 6 5 4 3 2 1

ACKNOWLEDGMENTS

Design and composition by: Stephen Strong
Cover design by: Jaclyn Smith

The authors would like to thank all the teachers and students around the world whose feedback has helped us to shape this series. We would also like to thank: Knut-Arne Iversen for his interview and photos, Liz Evans and Clive Salisbury for their photos of South America, Anna Kenyon for her interview, Felipe Edwards for advice on classic cars, Francesca Niesterowicz-Lawrence and Elizabeth Kirk for the Erasmus photo, and all members of the public who agreed to be filmed and interviewed.

The authors would also like to thank: all those at Oxford University Press (both in Oxford and around the world) and the design team who have contributed their skills and ideas to producing this course.

Finally, very special thanks from Clive to Maria Angeles, Lucia, and Eric, and from Christina to Cristina, for all their help and encouragement. Christina would also like to thank her children Joaquin, Marco, and Krysia for their constant inspiration.

The publisher and authors would also like to thank the following for their invaluable feedback on the materials: Vincent Collado Añón, Patrícia Brasileiro, Sybille Brinz, Kath Cicero, Louise Connolly, Kieran Donaghy, Alex Ellul, Carla Falcão, Emmanuel Godard, Gill Hamilton, Jane Hudson, David Jay, Rebecca Lennox, Joe Millanes, Marta Rudnicka, Anna Sliwa, and Andreza Valença.

The authors and publisher are grateful to those who have given permission to reproduce the following extracts and adaptations of copyright material: p. 35 "A Life in the Day: James Blunt" from Timesonline, Style and Culture. © NI Syndication 2007. Reproduced by kind permission of NI Syndication; p. 73 "The man who ran around the word" by Jürgen Ankenbrand. © Jürgen Ankenbrand. Reproduced by kind permission.

Although every effort has been made to trace and contact copyright holders before publication, this has not been possible in some cases. We apologize for any apparent infringement of copyright and if notified, the publisher will be pleased to rectify any errors or omissions at the earliest opportunity.

The publisher would like to thank the following for their kind permission to reproduce photographs and other copyright material: Alamy Images pp.5 (D Hurst/cup of coffee), 6 (Nic Cleave Photography/Temple at Nara, Dennis Cox/Blue Mosque, Art Kowalsky/Siena Cathedral, 9 (Sylvian Gradadam/Dim sum), 18 (Motoring Picture Library/Ferrari, 2CV), 19 (Mark Bourdillon/VW convertible), 22 (Mode Images Limited/keys, D Hurst/umbrella, Ian Nolan/ bag), 33 (Foodfolio/bread, olive oil, tomato), 39 (Carol and Mike Werner/coffee sign, Chuck Nacke/change sign, superclic/credit cards, RT signs/Wi-fi sign, Ted Pink/no football sign, 40 (Insurance/twenty pounds, fifty pence, Visions of America/Joe Sohm/twenty dollars, Eye-Stock/twenty euros, 41 (Chris Howes/Wild Places Photography/coffee), 43 (David R. Frazier Photolibrary/woman with sunglasses, 50 (Alex Segre/5th Avenue), 57 (Alan King/Blackpool beach), 63 (Arctic Images/Ragnar Th Sigurdsson), 71 (boringphotos/couple with policeman), 76 and 78 (Photos 12/Stephen Chow), 108 (Leonid Nyshko/sandwich, Tim Hill/sugar lumps and milk), 109 (mediacolor's/teacher, Roger Bamber/factory worker); Allstar and Sportsphoto pp.76 and 78 (Okasana Akinshina), 17 (Walt Disney/Pirates of the Caribbean/Jack Sparrow, 50 (Cinetext/Buena Vista/Sixth Sense poster), 76 and 78 (Gabriella Hámori); Jürgen Ankenbrand/J.A. Photography p.73; Catherine Blackie pp.5 (man and boys), 22 (boys); Casio p.9 (camera); Corbis pp.76 and 78 (Sygma./Ronald Siemoneit/Michael Zebrowski); Nick Cunard p.35 (James Blunt); Elkep Evi p.55 (hotel exterior); Getty Images pp.9 (Gary Gershoff/Bocelli, Ezra Shaw/American Football, English Football), 13 (Photographer's Choice/Ron Alston RM/American woman), 14 (Bruno Vincent), 25 (Jim Bastardo/listening to iPod, Kiyoshi Ota/Apple iPhone), 29 (Iconica/Jon Feingersh/meeting), 44 (Marty Melville/James Blunt, Dimitrios Kambouris/Calista Flockhart, Todd Williamson/Lucy Liu), 49 (Stephen Studd/The Forum, The Image Bank Simon Watson/couple), 53 (The Bridgman Art Library/Private Collection), 56 (Hulton Archive/Benidorm 1950's), 60 (Coldplay), 76 and 78 (Adriana Fonseca, Nanako Matsushima, Carlos Alvarez/Imanol Arias), 105 (Lifesize/boy, Altrendo/girl, Michael Cogliantry/man, DK Stock/woman), 108 (Michael Rosenfeld/Mackerel, Iconica Tom Grill/meat, Diana Miller/pasta, StockFood Creative/Ulrike Schmid/rice, Photographers Choice/Kevin Summers/eggs, Michael Rosenfeld/salad, StockFood Creative/potatoes, Photographer's Choice/Frans Lemmens/fruit, Smari/bread, StockFood Creative/Bodo A. Schieren/water, Ian O'Leary/orange juice, 109 (Image Bank/Mark Scott/assistant); Hammerfest Tourist Board p.36; Istockphoto p.10 (computer); Kamalame Cay p.55 (jetty); Knut-Arne Iversen p.37; Kobal Collection p.17 (Miramax/The Queen); Mercedes p.19 (Mercedes); Motoring Picture Library p.18 (Mazda, Ford Mustang); Oxford University Press pp.5 (Hotel sign), 39 (fSTop/no photography sign), 46 (Corbis/Digital Stock/Eiffel tower) 105 (Photodisc/family), 108 (Ingram/coffee); PA Photos pp.5 (ballroom dancing), 9 (Gisele Bündchen, The Rolling Stones, Sting, Jack Nicholson, Jennifer Aniston, Barbara Streisand, Morgan Freeman), 50 (man on moon); Photofusion p.109, David Hoffman/hospital ward); Photolibrary.com pp.9 (BMW logo, Warren Smith/TV, Cecile Parisi/Das Fotoarchiv/Disc Jockey), 13 (Jack Hollingsworth/Spanish girl), 23 (BananaStock/Mother and teenage children), 25 (Food Collection/glass of coke), 28 (Radius Images/girls chatting) 32 (Image Source/clock), 33 (Westend61/grapes; Tim Hill/fish), 39 (Photographer's Choice/Peter Dazeley/mobile phone sign, 40 Westend61/fifty cents euro), 43 Digital Vision/woman eating sandwich), 46 (BananaStock/man on telephone, BlueMoon Stock/girl on telephone), 77 and 79 (Image Source/clock), 105 (Stockbyte/four children, Rubberball Productions/Brother and sister), 108 (Fresh Food Images/cornflakes), 109 (© Image Source Black/Doctor, Digital Vision/nurse and waiter, Image Source Black/office, Botanica/man with laptop), 110 (Image Source/clock); Pictures Colour Library p.35 (Ibiza); Punchstock pp.108 (Image Source/butter, DK/Chocolate, DAJ/tea, 109 (Digital Vision/Student); Rex Features pp.7 (Sipa Press/Rodrigo Santoro), 17 (New Line/Everett Sex and the City, Miranda and Carrie, Walt Disney/BuenaVista/Everett/Pirates of the Caribbean/Captain Teague, Miramax/Everett/The Queen/Prince Philip, Sex and the City/Miranda and Carrie), 18 (Mini), 22 (Denis Closon/pen), 25 (reading a newspaper, cat), 44 (Stuart Clarke/Danny DeVito, Dave Allocca/Tina Turner), 50 (The Police), 56 (Benidorm today), 57 (Benidorm), 60 (CSU Archives/Everett Collection/Bob Dylan, Debra L. Rothenberg/Justin Timberlake, Unimedia South America/Shakira, Ken McKay/Enrique Iglesias, Sipa Press/Rolling Stones, Brian Rasic/Nelly Furtado, Sipa Press/Rihanna), 76 and 78 (Ricky Gervais, Camilla Morandi/Maria Grazia Cucinotta); Stephen Strong pp.25 (football), 31 (filofax); Volkswagen Press Office p.18 (VW); Image Source/AGE Fotostock: p 4 (Asian-American woman); Blend Images/Alamy: Andersen Ross p 4 (Hispanic woman); Stock Byte/Getty Images: p 5 (yellow cab); AGE Foto Stock/Art Life Images: José Mata p 6 (Mexican pyramid); Wireimage/Getty Images: Han Myung-Gu p 7 (Choi Ji-woo, Korean actress); Image Source/Superstock: p 8 (Japanese woman); Lifesize/Getty Images: Todd Warnock p 8 (Mexican woman); Transtock/Corbis: p 9 (Corvette); Hola Images/Art Life Images p 9 (burritos); Brand X Pictures/Jupiter Unlimited Images p 13 (Korean man); Photodisc/Superstock: p 15 (I.D. card); Everett Collection: p 17 (Luke Skyalker); mptvimages.com: Alex Bailey p 17 (Gemma Jones); Everett Collection: p 17 (Princess Leia); PhotoAlto/Art Life Images: Eric Audras p 20 (top left); Art Life Images: p 26 (American breakfast); epa/Corbis: Mario Guzman p 28 (museum); Masterfile: p 33 (Korean woman); Blend Images/OUP: p 33 (Korean man); Panoramic Images/Getty Images: p 39 (no parking sign); Axiom Photographic Agency/Getty Images: Paul Quayle p 39 (no swimming sign); Alamy: Andre Jenny p 39 (25 mph sign); OUP: p 40 (U.S. Quarter); iTravelstock collection/Clive Sawyer PCL/Art Life Images: p 47 (NYC Subway); PhotoAlto/Art Life Images: p 47 (man pushing stroller); dpa/Corbis: Peter Kneffel p 47 (scrape ice); Icon SMI/Corbis: Matt Brown p 47 (basketball on TV); Masterfile: p 47 (woman walking dog); Food Collection/Art Lfe Images: p 47 (slice of pizza); Courtesy of Poseidon Resorts; p 55 (Poseidon Underwater Hotel); Retna Ltd.: Brian Hineline p 60 (Avril Lavingne); Reuters: Jason Reed p 60 (Beyonce); Courtesy of Safari Land: p 63; Courtesy of Safari Land: p 63 (insert); Photos courtesy of the Soars p 65; Glowimages: Getty Images p 73 (Arequipa, Peru); Retna:© Sara De Boer p 76 (Jennifer Hudson); Graphi-Ogre/OUP: p 103 (flag of South Korea); Graphi-Ogre/OUP: p 103 (flag of Peru); ImageSource/Art Life Imags: p 104 (photo of couple); Masterfile: p 105 (two Asian female friends); Tongro Image Stock/Art Life Images: p 105 (wedding photo); Polka Dot Images/Jupiter Unlimited: p 108 (cheese); Comstock/Jupiter Unlimited: p 108 (glass of soda); Juice Images/AGE FotoStock: p 109 (a salesperson); RubberBall/Age Fotostock: p 109 (a lawyer); UpperCut Images/Art Life Images: p 109 (a policeman); Juice Images/AGE FotoStock: p 109 (in a store); Photolibrary /Alamy: Janine Wiedel p 109 (on the street).

Commissioned photography by: Gareth Boden pp. 20, 23 (Polish boy and sisters), 26 (Girl in café), 66; MM Studios pp.10 (DVD cover), 15, 22 (Japanese breakfast), 40 (New York Times, phone card, Sony memory card, and train ticket), 51 (calendar), 81, 104, 106, 108 (vegetables); Dennis Kitchen Studio p.17 (American family).

Illustrations by: The Art Market/Terry Kennett pp.54–55 (objects), 77 (two hotel rooms), 80 (two hotel rooms), 114; Thea Brine p.45; Cartoonstock/Ian Baker pp.16, 34, 38–39, 68 (picture of park), 69, 81 (picture of park); Phil Disley pp.24–25, 78, 80 (picture of bad hotel), 81 (a new haircut); Hand Made Maps pp.66–67, 68 (weather symbols), 70–71, 103 (countries), 115; Joanna Kerr p.35; Meiklejohn Illustration/Peter Ellis pp.4, 6, 8, 60; Ellis Nadler pronunciation symbols; Gavin Reece pp. 6, 48, 54 (couple at hotel), 58–59, 64, 104; Colin Shelbourn pp.89, 90–91, 100–101, 111; Kath Walker Illustration pp.10, 11, 12, 15, 30–31, 106–107, 112–113; Annabel Wright pp.27, 65, 72.